INCA KNITS

Designs Inspired by South American Traditions

MARIANNE ISAGER COLLECTION

INCA KNITS

Designs Inspired by South American Traditions

MARIANNE ISAGER COLLECTION

INTERWEAVE.

interweavestore.com

Editing Ann Budd
Translation Carol Huebscher Rhoades
Technical Editing Lori Gayle
Travel photos and diary notes Peder Baltzer Nielsen
Garment photos Carsten Ingemann
Detail photos Rikke Nygaard, Joe Coca
Illustrations Kirsten Toftegaard
Glossary illustrations Gayle Ford
Design Mark Lewis
Production Katherine Jackson

Interweave Press LLC
201 East Fourth Street
Loveland, CO 80537-5655 USA
interweavestore.com

Printed in China by Asia Pacific Offset.

Library of Congress Cataloging-in-Publication Data

Isager, Marianne, 1954-
Inca knits : designs inspired by South American
traditions / Marianne Isager, author.
p. cm.
Includes index.
ISBN 978-1-59668-116-3 (pbk.)
1. Knitting--Patterns. I. Title.
TT825.I827 2009
746.43'2041--dc22
2009003147

10 9 8 7 6 5 4 3 2 1

TABLE OF CONTENTS

INTRODUCTION

The designs for this book were inspired by a trip I made with my friend Peder through Chile, Bolivia, and Peru in 1994. I had been invited to teach knitting techniques in Chile and to help a woman's group sketch the patterns for their own designs. After the workshops, we traveled farther up the Chilean coast, ending up in Cusco, Peru.

Latin America is a paradise of patterns and colors. Woven ponchos worn as outer garments, lovely old pottery, colors in the landscape, vegetables in the marketplaces, boats on the beach—all of these images from the Incan empire contributed to the garments in this book.

When the first edition of *Inka* was published in Denmark in 1996, I began a long period of traveling to faraway places, including Greenland and Nepal. I also returned to the Andes Mountains to the island of Taquile in Lake Titicaca. Niels Boe, who worked for an organization that installed solar energy systems on the island, had a copy of the book and in no time, the men of the island joined him in knitting various projects. On Taquile, women traditionally weave while the men do the knitting. When I visited, mostly caps, headbands, and mittens were knitted. Today, they also knit sweaters from their own designs.

I hope that this book will inspire you to look for you own design inspirations, which can be found everywhere—from your own backyard to remote regions within your own country and abroad.

A gauge swatch is an important first step for the garments in this book. Before you begin a project, knit a gauge swatch to ensure that your garment will turn out the correct size, plus it will help you learn the stitch patterns on a manageable number of stitches.

MAIZE

The inspiration for this sweater was a fine antique Inca pot. The pattern on the side of the pot symbolizes a corn plant—an important component of the Incan diet.

Finished Size
About 37½ (41½, 45½)" (95 [105.5, 115.5] cm) bust circumference. Sweater shown photographed flat measures 41½" (105.5 cm).

Yarn
About 125 (150, 200) grams of a light color (A), 125 (100, 150) grams of a dark color (B), and small amounts of five contrasting colors (CC1, CC2, CC3, CC4, CC5) of fingering-weight (#1 Super Fine) yarn.

Shown here
For sweaters both on model and photographed flat: Isager Alpaca 2 (50% merino, 50% alpaca; 270 yd [247 m]/50 g): #2105 light gray heather (A), 3 (3, 4) skeins; #402 charcoal (CC2), #012 grayed olive (CC4), and #020 teal (CC5), 1 skein each. Isager Wool 1 (100% wool; 340 yd [310 m]/50 g): #052s plum heather (CC3), 1 skein.

For sweater on model: Isager Alpaca 2 (50% merino, 50% alpaca; 270 yd [247 m]/50 g): #011 steel blue (B), 3 (3, 4) skeins; #500 black (CC1), 1 skein.

For sweater photographed flat: Isager Alpaca 2 (50% merino, 50% alpaca; 270 yd [247 m]/50 g): #011 steel blue (used for both B and CC1), 3 (4, 4) skeins.

Needles
Body and sleeves—size U.S. 2 (3 mm): 16" and 24" (40 and 60 cm) circular (cir) and set of 4 or 5 double-pointed (dpn). *Facings*—size U.S. 1 (2.5 cm): 16" and 24" (40 and 60 cm) cir and set of 4 or 5 dpn. Adjust needle size if necessary to obtain the correct gauge.

Notions
Markers (m); tapestry needle; sharp-point sewing needle or sewing machine; contrasting basting thread; matching sewing thread.

Gauge
32 stitches and 34 rows/rounds = 4" (10 cm) in stranded two-color patterns on larger needle (see Notes on page 12).

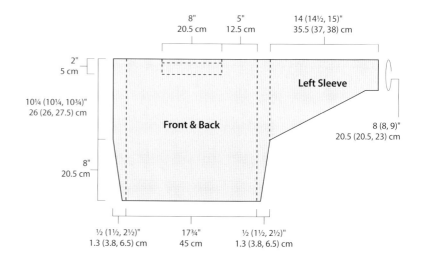

STITCH GUIDE

Vertical Stripes

(Multiple of 8 sts + 7)

All Rnds: K1 with A, k1 with B, k3 with A, *[k1 with B, k1 with A] 2 times, k1 with B, k3 with A; rep from * to last 2 sts, k1 with B, k1 with A.

Rep this rnd for patt.

Diagram labels:
- 8" / 20.5 cm
- 5" / 12.5 cm
- 14 (14½, 15)" / 35.5 (37, 38) cm
- 2" / 5 cm
- 10¼ (10¼, 10¾)" / 26 (26, 27.5) cm
- Left Sleeve
- Front & Back
- 8 (8, 9)" / 20.5 (20.5, 23) cm
- 8" / 20.5 cm
- ½ (1½, 2½)" / 1.3 (3.8, 6.5) cm
- 17¾" / 45 cm
- ½ (1½, 2½)" / 1.3 (3.8, 6.5) cm

NOTES

- The sweater is worked in stranded two-color knitting (see page 26) in one piece from cuff to cuff with a steek for the lower body opening. The front neck shaping is stitched and cut during finishing.

- The first sleeve is worked in the round, then a section is worked back and forth in rows to cast on stitches for the side of the body. The body is joined for working in the round again until it reaches the other side, then a second section is worked back and forth in rows to bind off stitches for the other side of the body. The stitches are joined for working in rounds again, and the second sleeve is worked in the round to the cuff.

- To adjust sleeve length, work more or fewer rounds before beginning the increases for the first sleeve. Make sure to add or remove the same number of rounds after completing the decreases for the second sleeve.

- Change needle size if necessary to maintain the same gauge when working back and forth in rows as when working in rounds. Similarly, you may find that you need to change needle size in order to maintain the same gauge for the vertical stripes as well as the charted maize and cross patterns.

- The solid-color stripes between the charted patterns of the center body are worked using CC1, CC2, CC3, CC4, and CC5 randomly. For each 9-round stripe, use each color for at least 1 of the 9 rounds but do not use any color for more than 3 rounds in succession. For the 2-round stripes, work 1 round each of two different colors.

- The sweater shown photographed flat uses the same color for both B and CC1.

RIGHT SLEEVE

With CC3 and smaller dpn, CO 64 (64, 72) sts. Place marker (pm) and join for working in rnds, being careful not to twist sts. Work in St st (knit every rnd) until piece measures ¾" (2 cm) from CO. Purl 1 rnd for turning ridge, then knit 1 rnd. Change to larger dpn.

Next rnd: Work 63 (63, 71) sts in Vertical Stripes patt (see Stitch Guide), knit last st with B for "seam" st.

Keeping last st of rnd in B, work even in patt until piece measures 1¼ (1¾, 2¼)" (3.2 [4.5, 5.5] cm) from turning ridge or desired length (see Notes). Cont in patt with seam st in B and *at the same time* inc 1 st each side of seam st every 3 rnds 8 times, then every 2 rnds 42 times, working new sts into stripe patt and changing to 16" (40 cm) cir needle in larger size when there are too many sts to fit on dpns—164 (164, 172) sts.

Next rnd. Removing markers as you come to them, M1 (see Glossary) with B, work in established patt to last st, k1 with B—165 (165, 173) sts; 1 st in B at each end of rnd; piece measures about 14 (14½, 15)" (35.5 [37, 38] cm) from turning ridge.

Mark center (shoulder line) of last rnd completed with waste yarn to indicate end of sleeve.

RIGHT SIDE

Note: Cont Vertical Stripes patt in rows by working existing sts in St st (knit on RS; purl on WS) using matching colors and work new CO sts into established stripe patt.

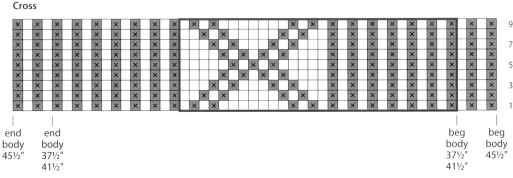

Cross

9
7
5
3
1

end body 45½" | end body 37½" 41½" | beg body 37½" 41½" | beg body 45½"

Next row: (RS) Work in patt to end, then use the backward-loop method (see Glossary) to CO 32 (13, 13) sts in patt at end of row, turn—197 (178, 186) sts.

Next row: (WS) Work new sts in patt, work to end, then use the backward-loop method to CO 32 (13, 13) sts in patt at end of row, turn—229 (191, 199) sts.

Working back and forth in rows in this manner, work 2 (8, 8) more rows, CO 32 (13, 13) sts at end of first 2 (6, 6) rows, then CO 12 sts at end of next 0 (2, 2) rows, changing to 24" (60 cm) cir needle in larger size when necessary—293 (293, 301) sts; piece measures about ½ (1¼, 1¼)" (1.3 [3.2, 3.2] cm) from end of sleeve.

CENTER BODY

With A, work 1 RS row even in patt, pm, then use the backward-loop method to CO 3 steek sts for lower body steek onto righthand needle, pm, and join for working in rnds again—296 (296, 304) sts. On the foll rnds, work the 3 steek sts in a solid color, 1×1

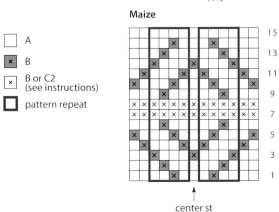

Maize

15
13
11
9
7
5
3
1

☐ A

☒ B

☒ B or C2 (see instructions)

☐ pattern repeat

center st

checkerboard patt, or stripes, as you prefer in order to distinguish them from the patt sts. Work 0 (2, 10) rnds even in patt—piece measures about ½ (1½, 2½)" (1.3 [3.8, 6.5] cm) from end of right sleeve.

Next rnd: Establish patt from Rnd 1 of Maize chart by working 2 sts before first patt rep box once, work first 4-st patt 36 (36, 37) times, work center st once, work second 4-st patt 36 (36, 37) times, work 2 sts after second patt rep box once, work 3 steek sts.

Work Rnds 2–15 of Maize chart, using C2 for Rnd 7 and B for Rnd 8. With CC, work a 2-rnd stripe (see Notes).

Next rnd: Work Rnd 1 of Cross chart over 293 (293, 301) sts, work 3 steek sts.

Work Rnds 2–9 of chart. *With CC, work a 9-rnd stripe, then work Rnds 1–9 of Cross chart; rep from * 5 more times. With CC, work a 2-rnd stripe, then knit 1 rnd with A. Work Rnds 1–15 of Maize chart, using B for Rnd 7 and C2 for Rnd 8—152 rnds in chart section of center body; piece measures 17¾" (45 cm) from beg of chart patts for all sizes and 18¼ (19¼, 20¼)" (46.5 [49, 51.5] cm) from end of right sleeve. Matching the same arrangement of the stripes as at the end of the right side, work Vertical Stripes patt with steek sts for 0 (2, 10) rnds. Work 1 rnd in patt to last 3 sts, BO 3 steek sts, break yarn— 293 (293, 301) sts; piece measures about 18¼ (19½, 21½)" (46.5 [49.5, 54.5] cm) from end of right sleeve.

LEFT SIDE
With RS facing, rejoin yarn to beg of sts on needle. Working stripe patt back and forth in rows, BO 12 sts at beg of next 0 (2, 2) rows, then BO 32 (13, 13) sts at beg of next 4 (8, 8) rows—165 (165, 173) sts rem. Mark center (shoulder line) of last row completed to indicate beg of left sleeve—piece measures about 18¾ (20¾, 22¾)" (47.5 [52.5, 58] cm) between sleeve markers.

LEFT SLEEVE
Rejoin for working in the rnd.

Next rnd: K2tog at beg of rnd in color to maintain patt, work in patt to last st, k1 with B to re-establish seam st—164 (164, 172) sts.

Cont in patt and *at the same time* dec 1 st on each side of seam st every 2 rnds 42 times, then every 3 rnds 8 times, changing to 16" (40 cm) cir needle in larger size, then larger dpn as necessary—64 (64, 72) sts rem. Work even in patt until sleeve measures 14 (14½, 15)" (35.5 [37, 38] cm) from marker at start of left sleeve, or desired length to match right sleeve. Change to CC3 and smaller dpn. Knit 1 rnd, then purl 1 rnd for turning ridge. Work in St st until piece measures ¾" (2 cm) from turning ridge. BO all sts.

Back

ANDES

A clay pot with a little triangle
pattern in various colors inspired the
geometric design in this pullover.

Finished Size

About 34½ (39, 46, 53½)" (87.5 [99 117, 136] cm) chest/bust circumference. Sweater shown photographed flat measures 46" (117 cm).

Yarn

About 175 (200, 225, 260) grams of dark main color (A), 50 (60, 70, 80) grams of medium secondary color (B), 60 (65, 70, 75) grams accent color (C), and 25 (30, 35, 40) grams of another accent color (D) of fingering-weight (#1 Super Fine) yarn.

Shown here

For sweaters both on model and photographed flat: Isager Wool 1 (100% wool; 340 yd [310 m]/50 g): #055 plum (A), 4 (4, 5, 6) skeins, Isager Alpaca 2 (50% merino, 50% alpaca; 270 yd [247 m]/50 g): #014 orange (C), 2 skeins for all sizes; and #23 blue (D), 1 skein for all sizes.

For sweater on model: Isager Wool 1 (100% wool; 340 yd [310 m]/50 g): #052s plum heather (B), 1 (2, 2, 2) skeins.

For sweater photographed flat: Isager Alpaca 2 (50% merino, 50% alpaca; 270 yd [247 m]/50 g): wine (B, discontinued), 1 (2, 2, 2) skeins.

Needles

Size U.S. 2 (3 mm): One 16" and two 24" (40 and 60 cm) circular (cir). Adjust needle size if necessary to obtain the correct gauge.

Notions

Stitch holders; removable markers or waste yarn; markers (m); tapestry needle.

Gauge

26 stitches and 52 rows = 4" (10 cm) in garter stitch; 28 stitches and 40 rows = 4" (10 cm) in stockinette-stitch colorwork pattern from chart.

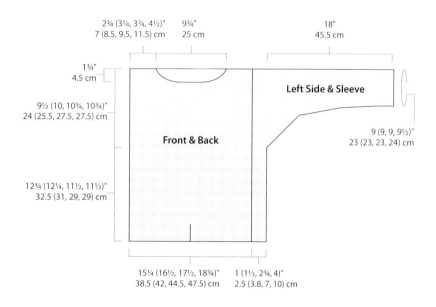

2¾ (3¼, 3¾, 4½)" 9¾"
7 (8.5, 9.5, 11.5) cm 25 cm

18"
45.5 cm

1¾"
4.5 cm

Left Side & Sleeve

9½ (10, 10¾, 10¾)"
24 (25.5, 27.5, 27.5) cm

Front & Back

9 (9, 9, 9½)"
23 (23, 23, 24) cm

12¾ (12¼, 11½, 11½)"
32.5 (31, 29, 29) cm

15¼ (16½, 17½, 18¾)" 1 (1½, 2¾, 4)"
38.5 (42, 44.5, 47.5) cm 2.5 (3.8, 7, 10) cm

Knit the gauge swatch in the color pattern.

NOTES

- The front and back are worked back and forth in rows, beginning with a split lower border and ending at the shoulder line. After joining the shoulders, stitches for the side panels and sleeve are picked up along the selvedges of the back and front and worked downward to the cuffs.

- For the garter-stitch lower borders, you may find it helpful to mark one side of the garter-stitch fabric as the right side.

- For the charted section of the back and front, knit the first and last stitches of every row; these selvedge stitches are not shown on the chart. For chart rows that contain two colors, knit the first and last stitches with both colors held together.

- The side panels and sleeves are worked in intarsia (see page 53) using a separate ball of color B for the center stitches and two separate balls of color A for the stitches on each side. Twist the yarns at the color changes to avoid leaving holes.

- When picking up stitches along the edges of body for the side panels, pick up one stitch in from the edge so the garter selvedge stitches of the body do not show on the RS of the garment.

BACK

With A and shorter cir needle, CO 50 (54, 57, 61) sts. Work in garter st (knit every row) until piece measures 2¼" (5.5 cm) from CO, ending with a RS row (see Notes). Break yarn and set aside. With A and longer cir needle, work another piece in the same manner, but do not break yarn.

Joining row: (WS) Using longer cir needle already holding second border sts, knit across second border sts, then with WS facing, knit across 50 (54, 57, 61) first border sts—100 (108, 114, 122) sts.

Change to B and work 2 rows in St st (knit on RS, purl on WS). Change to A and knit 1 RS row, then knit 1 WS row inc 7 (7, 9, 9) sts evenly spaced—107 (115, 123, 131) sts; piece measures about 2½" (6.5 cm) from CO.

Set-up row: (RS) K1 (selvedge st, see Notes), work Row 1 of Andes chart over center 105 (113, 121, 129) sts, k1 (selvedge st).

Keeping 1 garter selvedge st at each side, work Rows 2–30 of chart once, then rep Rows 1–30 of chart 4 times, then work Rows 1–26 once more—176 chart rows total; piece measures about 20" (51 cm) from CO. Change to A and knit 1 RS row, then knit 1 WS row dec 7 (7, 9, 9) sts evenly spaced—100 (108, 114, 122) sts rem. Knit 26 more rows with A—28 rows and 14 garter ridges completed from end of chart patt; piece measures about 2¼" (5.5 cm) above last chart row, and 22¼" (56.5 cm) from CO. Place 18 (22, 25, 29) sts at each side on separate holders for shoulders and place center 64 sts on a third holder for back neck.

Back

FRONT

Work as for back until Andes chart has been completed—107 (115, 123, 131) sts; piece measures about 20" (51 cm) from CO. Change to A and knit 1 RS row, then knit 1 WS row dec 7 (7, 9, 9) sts evenly spaced—100 (108, 114, 122) sts. With A, knit 4 more rows—piece measures about 20½" (52 cm) from CO.

Shape Neck

Mark center 20 sts with removable marker or waste yarn—40 (44, 47, 51) sts on each side of marked center sts. Work short-rows (see page 147) with A to shape each side of neck separately as foll.

Left Front

Short-row 1: (RS) K40 (44, 47, 51) to marked center sts, yo, turn.

Even-numbered Short-rows 2–18: (WS) Knit to end.

Short-row 3: Knit to 6 sts before marked center sts, yo, turn.

Short-row 5: Knit to 4 sts before previous turning point, yo, turn.

Short-rows 7, 9, 11, 13, and 15: Knit to 2 sts before previous turning point, yo, turn.

Short-rows 17 and 19: Knit to 1 st before previous turning point, yo, turn.

Short-row 20: K18 (22, 25, 29) to end.

Next row: (RS) Knit across all sts, working each turning point yo along left front neck shaping tog with the st after it as k2tog.

Right Front

Short-row 1: (WS) K40 (44, 47, 51) to marked center sts, yo, turn.

Even-numbered Short-rows 2–18: Work as for left front neck; even-numbered rows will be RS rows and odd-numbered rows will be WS rows.

Short-row 3: Knit to 6 sts before marked center sts, yo, turn.

Short-row 5: Knit to 4 sts before previous turning point, yo, turn.

Short-rows 7, 9, 11, 13, and 15: Knit to 2 sts before previous turning point, yo, turn.

Short-rows 17 and 19: Knit to 1 st before previous turning point, yo, turn.

Short-row 20: (RS) K18 (22, 25, 29) to end.

Next row: (WS) Knit across all sts, working each turning point yo along right front neck shaping tog with the st after it as ssk (see Glossary)—28 rows and 14 garter ridges completed from end of chart patt at shoulders; piece measures same as back at shoulder line.

Place 18 (22, 25, 29) sts at each side on separate holders for shoulders and place center 64 sts on a third holder for front neck.

LEFT SIDE AND SLEEVE

Join 18 (22, 25, 29) shoulder sts of back and front using the three-needle bind-off method (see Glossary)—64 held sts rem at center back and front.

Side Panel

With B, longer cir needle, and RS of front facing, pick up and knit 130 sts along left front side from CO edge to top front chart row (see Notes), pm, 15 sts along front garter st section to shoulder join, 15 sts along back garter st section to top back chart row, pm, then 130 sts along left back side to CO edge—290 sts total. Work 5 rows in St st, beg and ending with a WS row. Break yarn. With WS facing, slip the second longer cir needle into each purl bump of the pick-up row; these loops are just picked up and placed on the needle, not picked up and knitted—290 picked-up loops on second cir needle. Hold needles tog and parallel with RS facing, live sts on front (working) needle, and picked-up loops on back needle. With A, *insert right-hand tip of working needle into first st on both needles and k2tog (1 st from each needle);* rep from * to * to first m, with B rep from * to * across 30 center sts, then with a separate ball of A rep from * to * from second m to end—290 sts on working needle; all picked-up loops have been joined; 30 center sts in B; 130 sts at each side in A. Using the intarsia method (see Notes), work sts in their matching colors in garter st until piece measures 1 (1½, 2¾, 4)" (2.5 [3.8, 7, 10] cm) from pick-up row, ending with a WS row. With RS facing, place the first and last 83 (79, 75, 75) sts on separate holders for sides—124 (132, 140, 140) sts rem; 30 center sts in B, 47 (51, 55, 55) sts at each side in A. Break color A attached to held sts at lower left front.

Sleeve

With RS facing, rejoin A to beg of sts on needle.

Next row: (RS) Working in garter st intarsia as established, k1, k2tog, knit to end—1 st dec'd.

Rep the last row 59 more times—64 (72, 80, 80) sts rem; piece measures about 5½ (6, 7¼, 8½)" (14 (15, 18.5, 21.5] cm) from pick-up row.

Next row: (RS) Cont in garter st intarsia, k1, k2tog, knit to last 3 sts, ssk, k1—2 sts dec'd.

Legend

- ⬛ A: k on RS; p on WS
- ▪ A: k on WS
- ⊙ B: k on RS; p on WS
- ◉ B: k on WS
- Ι C: k on RS; p on WS
- + C: k on WS
- ✕ D: k on RS; p on WS
- ☐ pattern repeat

Andes

Cont as established, dec 1 st each end of needle in this manner every 7½ (2½, 1, 1)" (19 [6.5, 2.5, 2.5] cm) 1 (3, 7, 7) more time(s), ending with a RS dec row—60 (64, 64, 64) sts rem. Work even if necessary for your size until piece measures about 13 (13½, 14¾, 16)" (33 [34.5, 37.5, 40.5] cm) from pick-up row. **Note:** Work sleeve welt using ball of

A attached to end of last RS row completed; do not break off center ball of B or the other ball of A. With A attached at beg of next WS row, work 5 rows in St st, beg and ending with a WS row. Break off ball of A used for welt. With WS facing, slip the second longer cir needle into each purl bump of the first St st row (5 rows below the needle); these loops are just picked up and placed on the needle, not picked up and knitted—60 (64, 64, 64) picked-up loops on second cir needle. Hold needles tog and parallel with RS facing, live sts on front (working) needle, and picked-up loops on back needle. With A still attached to piece, *insert right-hand tip of working needle into first st on both needles and k2tog (1 st from each needle);* rep from * to * to first m, with B, rep from * to * across 30 center sts, then rejoin the second ball of A and rep from * to * from second m to end—60 (64, 64, 64) sts on working needle; all picked-up loops have been joined; 30 center sts in B; 15 (17, 17, 17) sts at each side in A. Cont in garter st intarsia as established, dec 1 st at each end of needle every 8th row 1 (3, 3, 1) time(s)—58 (58, 58, 62) sts. Work even until piece measures 18" (45.5 cm) for all sizes from where side sts were placed on holder, and about 19 (19½, 20¾, 22)" (48.5 [49.5, 52.5, 56] cm) from pick-up row, ending with a WS row. BO all sts in their matching colors.

RIGHT SIDE AND SLEEVE

With B, longer cir needle, and RS of back facing, pick up and knit 130 sts along right back side from CO edge to top back chart row, pm, 15 sts along back garter st section to shoulder join, 15 sts along front garter st section to top front chart row, pm, then 130 sts along right front side to CO edge—290 sts total. Work side panel and sleeve as for left side.

FINISHING

Carefully steam-press pieces to measurements under a damp cloth. **Note:** Right side panel and sleeve are not shown on schematic.

Neckband

Place 128 held neck sts on shorter cir needle and join A with RS facing to right shoulder, join at start of back neck sts. Pm and join for working in rnds. Work garter st in the rnd (knit 1 rnd, purl 1 rnd) until neckband measures 1¾" (4.5 cm), ending with a knit rnd. Change to B and purl 1 rnd for neckband turning ridge. Work in St st with B (knit every rnd) until neckband facing measures 1¾" (4.5 cm) from turning ridge. BO all sts loosely with B. With B, shorter cir needle, and beg at one side of neckband, pick up and knit 128 sts from the row of purl bumps along the turning ridge. Pm and join for working in rnds. Work in St st with B for ¾" (2 cm) for rolled neck edging. BO all sts. Fold neckband facing to WS and sew invisibly in place with A threaded on a tapestry needle.

Join 83 (79, 75, 75) held sts at each side of back and front using the three-needle bind-off method. With A threaded on a tapestry needle, sew sleeve seams using mattress st (see Glossary). Weave in loose ends.

STRANDED TWO-COLOR KNITTING

Stranded two-color knitting, also called jacquard or Fair Isle knitting, involves working with two colors at the same time, although in such a way that one color is stranded across the back (wrong side) of the work while the other color is being knitted. The keys to success are even tension (the unworked strands must have the same widthwise tension as the knitting) and consistent use of the two colors so that one color is the dominant color throughout.

Dominant Color

The manner in which you hold the two yarns in stranded knitting may result in the stitches of one color being slightly larger than the stitches of the other, causing them to "pop" out from the background on the right side of the work. The slightly more prominent stitches are said to be in the dominant color.

For best results, use the Continental method of knitting and hold both yarns in your left hand. Hold one color over your index finger and the other over both your index and middle fingers (Figure 1). It is worthwhile to learn this method as it offers several advantages:

- The two strands are not in contact with each other and therefore cannot tangle.

- The strand that is not worked (the "float") will have the same tension as the strand that is knitted, therefore the fabric is less likely to pucker.

- The strand that lies closest to the knitting (the one that lies over just your index finger), will be the primary

strand in the pattern. The stitches made with this strand will be slightly larger than the others and therefore, this strand is designated the dominant color.

Practice Two-Color Stranded Knitting

To practice, you will need needles and two colors of yarn—one light and one dark. Cast on 8 stitches with the light yarn. Place the yarns over the index and middle fingers of your left hand as shown in Figure 1 so that the light yarn is in the dominant position—farthest from your fingertip and draped over just your index finger. Alternate one stitch of each color in stockinette stitch as follows:

Right-Side Rows

Step 1: Knit the first stitch with both colors held together.

Step 2: Insert the right needle through the second stitch and knit it with the light yarn (Figure 2).

Step 3: Insert the right needle through the next stitch, bring it over the light yarn, and knit the stitch with the dark yarn (Figure 3).

Alternate Steps 2 and 3 (working one stitch each of each color) in this manner to the last stitch. Knit the last stitch with both colors held together (Figure 4).

Wrong-Side Rows

To keep the light yarn dominant on the right side of the piece while working wrong-side rows, rearrange the yarns in your left hand so that the dark yarn is

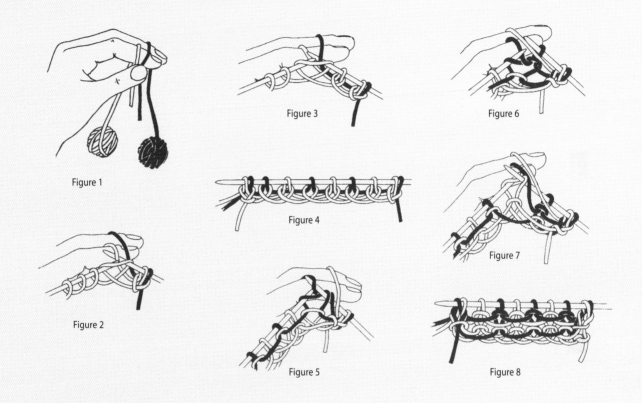

Figure 1

Figure 2

Figure 3

Figure 4

Figure 5

Figure 6

Figure 7

Figure 8

positioned as the dominant color—so that the dark color is farthest from your fingertips and is draped over just your index finger.

Step 1: Knit the first stitch with both colors held together.

Step 2: Insert the needle under both yarns, then purl the next stitch with the dark yarn (Figure 5), pulling the stitch under the light yarn so that the light yarn remains on the wrong side of the work (Figure 6).

Step 3: Insert the needle under both yarns, purl the next stitch with the light yarn, catching the light yarn over the top of the dark yarn and pulling the stitch under the dark yarn so that the dark yarn remains on the wrong side of the work (Figure 7).

Alternate Steps 2 and 3 to the last stitch. Knit the last stitch with both colors held together (Figure 8).

To work stranded two-color knitting in rounds, the right side of the work will always face you and there will be no edge stitches. Therefore, you will always hold the two yarns the same way and will work every stitch with just one color.

CIRCLES

The pattern of circles on the side of an ancient Peruvian pot inspired the design for this reversible double-knit sweater.

Finished Size
About 40 (52)" (101.5 [132] cm) chest/bust circumference with fronts overlapped by one block in center. Sweater shown photographed flat measures 40" (101.5 cm) **Note:** Adjust amount of overlap to accommodate smaller or larger sizes.

Yarn
About 200 (350) grams of a dark color (A), 100 (175) grams of a light color (B), and 150 (250) grams of a medium color (C) of fingering-weight (#1 Super Fine) yarn. About 175 (300) grams of a dark color (D), 75 (150) grams of a bright color (E), 25 (40) grams of a light color (F), and 50 (90) grams of a medium color (G) of the same or slightly thinner fingering-weight (#1 Super Fine) or laceweight (#0 Lace) yarn. **Note:** Yarns are used with two strands held together throughout.

Shown here:
Isager Alpaca 2 (50% merino, 50% alpaca; 270 yd [247 m]/50 g): #011 steel blue (A), 4 (7) skeins; #2105 light gray heather (B), 2 (4) skeins; #408 medium brown heather (C), 3 (5) skeins.

Isager Wool 1 (100% wool; 340 yd [310 m]/50 g): #30 black (D), 4 (6) skeins; #1s rust heather (E), 2 (3) skeins; #10s light blue heather (F), 1 skein for both sizes; #52s plum heather (G), 1 (2) skein(s).

Needles
Size U.S. 7 (4.5 mm): three 16" and one 32" (40 and 80 cm) circular (cir). Adjust needle size if necessary to obtain the correct gauge.

Notions
Stitch holders; cable needle (cn); tapestry needle.

Gauge
20 stitches (one layer) and 25 rows = 4" (10 cm) counted on one face of double knitting with two yarns held together (see Notes on pages 30–31); 25 (33) stitches (one layer) and 30 (40) rows in double knitting from Large Circle chart measure about 5 (6½)" (12.5 [16.5] cm) wide and 4¾ (6½)" (12 [16.5] cm) high; 13 (17) stitches (one layer) and 14 (18) rows in double knitting from Small Circle chart measure about 2½ (3½)" (6.5 [9] cm) wide and 2¼ (2¾)" (5.5 [7] cm) high.

STITCH GUIDE

Double Knitting Decrease

Sl the knit st of the knit/purl pair to be dec'd temporarily to right-hand needle as if to purl with yarn in back (pwise wyb). Sl the purl st of the same knit/purl pair onto cable needle (cn) and hold in back. Return the slipped knit st to the left needle and with both colors held in back, knit the two knit sts tog with color of double-knitting RS layer. Return the purl st from cn to the left-hand needle and with both colors held in front, purl the two purl sts tog with color of the double-knitting WS layer—2 sts total and 1 knit/purl pair dec'd.

NOTES

- The jacket body is worked back and forth in rows in one piece to the armholes, then divided for working the upper back and fronts separately. The sleeves are worked separately, back and forth in rows, from the top down to make length adjustments easier.

- Add or remove blocks at the end of the sleeves to adjust length; every block added or removed will lengthen or shorten the sleeve by about 2¼ (2¾)" (5.5 [7] cm). If you are making shorter sleeves, place the decrease rows closer together in order to complete all the required decreases by the time the sleeve reaches the desired length.

- Each color used in this project is made up of two different yarns held together that are indicated by their letter names. B/E, for example, means to work with one strand each of B and E held together.

- Double knitting (see page 36) forms two layers of knitted fabric at the same time. The stitches of the two layers alternate on the needle. Using two colors creates a reversible color pattern as you interchange the yarns for the two layers.

- The charts show the RS face of the double-knitting fabric. Each row on the chart is one row of knitting for both layers. One grid square of the chart represents two stitches on the needle—a knit stitch for the side of the fabric facing toward you (the "front" of the work at that moment) and a purl stitch for the side of the fabric facing away from you (the "back" of the work at that moment). The knit stitch forms the right side of the front fabric and the purl stitch forms the wrong side of the back fabric.

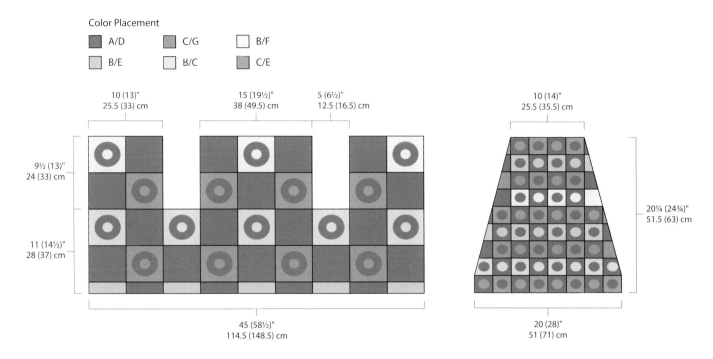

Color Placement

- ■ A/D
- ■ C/G
- □ B/F
- ▨ B/E
- ▨ B/C
- ■ C/E

10 (13)"
25.5 (33) cm

15 (19½)"
38 (49.5) cm

5 (6½)"
12.5 (16.5) cm

10 (14)"
25.5 (35.5) cm

9½ (13)"
24 (33) cm

11 (14½)"
28 (37) cm

20¼ (24¾)"
51.5 (63) cm

45 (58½)"
114.5 (148.5) cm

20 (28)"
51 (71) cm

- When working double knitting from the charts, on RS rows work the knit stitch of each pair in the color shown on the chart holding the unused color in back, then work the purl stitch of each pair in the opposite color holding the unused color in front. On WS rows, work the knit stitch of each pair in the opposite color and the purl stitch in the color shown on the chart.

- For the Large Circle chart, work the 25 stitches and 30 rows as outlined for the smaller size, beginning the chart with Row 6 worked as a RS row and ending with Row 35 worked as a WS row, for a total of 30 rows in each block. For the larger size, work all 33 stitches and 40 rows of the chart, working odd-numbered rows as RS rows and even-numbered rows as WS rows.

- For the Small Circle chart, work the 13 stitches and 14 rows as outlined for the smaller size, working Rows 3–16, for a total of 14 rows in each block. For the larger size, work all 17 stitches and 18 rows of the chart. For both sizes, odd-numbered rows are RS rows and even-numbered rows are WS rows.

- Where selvedge stitches are used, slip the first stitch (all four strands) as if to purl with both colors in front (pwise wyf) and knit the last stitch with both colors (all four strands) held together.

- Although the finished garment will be reversible, one side has been designated as the right side for working the project. The diagram shows the color placement in each pattern block as it will appear on the right side of the fabric. The back photographed on page 32 shows the garment inside out.

Back, viewed inside out

LOWER BODY

With longer cir needle and colors B/E and A/D, CO 227 (299) sts with all 4 strands held tog. **Set-up row:** (WS) Sl all 4 strands of first CO loop as if to purl with both colors in front (pwise wyf), *[with A/D knit the A/D loops of the CO st and leave it on the left needle, bring both yarns to front, then with B/E purl the B/E loops of the same CO st, sl the CO st off the left needle, and take both yarns to the back] 25 (33) times, then [with B/E knit the B/E loops of the CO st and leave it on the left needle, bring both yarns to front, then with A/D purl the A/D loops of the same CO st, sl the CO st off the left needle, and take both yarns to the back] 25 (33) times; rep from * 3 more

times, [with A/D knit the A/D loops of the CO st and leave it on the left needle, bring both yarns to front, then with B/E purl the B/E loops of the same CO st, sl the CO st off the left needle, and take both yarns to the back] 25 (33) times, knit last st with both colors (all 4 strands) held tog—452 (596) sts total; 9 double-knitting blocks with 25 (33) knit/purl pairs in each block; 1 selvedge st at each side.

Next row: (RS) Sl the first st pwise wyf, work each 25 (33)-st block in double knitting using its matching color, knit last st with both colors held tog. Rep the last row until piece measures 1½" (3.8 cm) from CO as shown on schematic on page 31, ending with a WS row. Cut off B/E and join C/G.

Next row: (RS) Sl 1 pwise wyf, *work 25 (33) sts in solid-color double knitting with RS color shown, work 25 (33) sts in patt from Row 6 (1) of Large Circle chart (see Notes); rep from * to last block, work 25 (33) sts in solid-color double knitting with colors as shown, k1.

Cont in patts until Row 35 (40) of chart has been completed—30 (40) rows total in this tier of blocks; piece measures about 6¼ (8)" (16 [20.5] cm) from CO. Cut C/G and join B/C. Work 30 (40) rows for the next tier of blocks as shown—piece measures about 11 (14½)" (28 [37] cm) from CO.

DIVIDE FOR FRONT AND BACK

Cut off B/C and join C/E in preparation to beg the next tier of blocks. On the next RS row, sl 1 pwise wyf, work two 25 (33)-st right-front blocks in patt for next tier as shown, BO 50 (66) sts of next block for right armhole by working each knit/purl pair as k2tog 25 (33) times with both colors (all 4 strands) held tog and working the first st of the foll block using one color (2 strands) before BO the last right armhole st. Work in patt to end of three 25 (33)-st back blocks as shown. BO next 25 (33)-st block for left armhole same as for right armhole. Work two 25 (33)-st left front blocks in patt, k1 for selvedge st. Place 101 (133) sts of right front on holder (2 blocks plus 1 selvedge st), then place 150 (198) sts of back on separate holder (3 blocks).

LEFT FRONT

Cont in established patt with A/D and C/E on 101 (133) left front sts, working a selvedge st at left front edge (end of RS rows; beg of WS rows), but do not work a selvedge st at the armhole edge (beg of RS rows; end of WS rows). The two double-knitting layers rem unjoined at the armhole edge so the sleeve can be inserted between them during finishing. Work in patt until two tiers of blocks have been completed above where fronts and back divided—armhole measures about 9½ (13)" (24 [33] cm). Place sts on holder.

BACK

Return 150 (198) held back sts to longer cir needle and rejoin A/D and C/E with WS facing. Do not re-establish selvedge sts at armhole edges; as for the left front, the two double-knitting layers rem unjoined at the armhole edges to accommodate the sleeves during

finishing. Work in patt until two tiers of blocks have been completed above where fronts and back divided—armholes measure same as left front. Place sts on holder.

RIGHT FRONT

Return 101 (133) sts held right front sts to longer cir needle and rejoin A/D and C/E with WS facing. As for left front and back, do not work a selvedge st at the armhole edge (beg of WS rows; end of RS rows). Work in patt until two tiers of blocks have been completed above where fronts and back divided—armhole measures same as left front and back. Place sts on holder.

JOIN FRONT AND BACK AT SHOULDERS

Divide 50 (66) sts of right front shoulder (one block at armhole edge) alternately onto two shorter cir needles, placing the knit sts of each knit/purl pair on one needle and the purled sts of each pair on the other—25 (33) sts on each needle. Divide 50 (66) sts of right back shoulder in the same manner on rem shorter and longer cir needles. Hold pieces with RS touching and WS facing out. Working with needle tip of longer needle, use the three-needle bind-off method (see Glossary) to join shoulder sts from RS double-knitting layers of back and front tog. With WS of garment facing and matching colors threaded on a tapestry needle, use the Kitchener st (see Glossary) to graft shoulder sts from WS double-knitting layers tog. Join left shoulder sts in the same

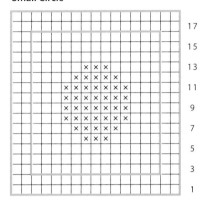

Large Circle

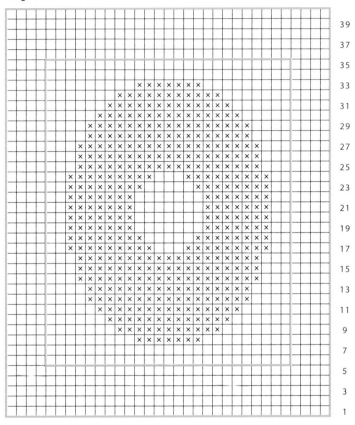

39	
37	
35	
33	
31	
29	
27	
25	
23	
21	
19	
17	
15	
13	
11	
9	
7	
5	
3	
1	

Small Circle

17
15
13
11
9
7
5
3
1

× circle color

☐ background color

☐ size 40"

☐ size 52"

manner—51 (67) sts at outer edge of each front and 50 (66) sts at center back rem on holders.

SLEEVES

With longer cir needle and colors A/D and C/E, CO 104 (136) sts with all 4 strands held tog.

Set-up row: (WS) *[With A/D knit the A/D loops of the CO st and leave it on the left needle, bring both yarns to front, then with C/E purl the C/E loops of the same CO st, sl the CO st off the left needle, and take both yarns to the back] 13 (17) times, then [with C/E knit the C/E loops of the CO st and leave it on the left needle, bring both yarns to front, then with A/D purl the A/D loops of the same CO st, sl the CO st off the left needle, and take both yarns to the back] 13 (17) times; rep from * 3 more times—208 (272) sts total; 8

double-knitting blocks with 13 (17) knit/purl pairs in each block.

Note: The sleeve is worked without selvedge sts; the two double-knitting layers rem unjoined at each side so the sleeve can be invisibly seamed on both sides of the fabric during finishing.

Next row: (RS) Work each 13 (17)-st block in double-knitting patt from Row 1 of Small Circle chart (see Notes).

Cont in patt until Row 14 (18) of chart has been completed; piece measures about 2¼ (2¾)" (5.5 [7] cm) from CO. Cont in patt, changing colors as shown on diagram and *at the same time* beg on Row 1 of the second tier of blocks, dec 1 knit/purl pair at each end of needle (4 sts total, 2 sts from each end) every 4 rows 26 (34) times—104 (136) sts; 4 double-knitting blocks with 13 (17) knit/purl pairs in each block. Cont even in patt until nine 14 (18)-row tiers have been completed from beg, or to desired length (see Notes)—piece measures about 20¼ (24¾)" (51.5 [63] cm) from CO. If a partial block does not contain enough sts to work complete small circle motif, work the sts in the background color as shown on schematic. BO all sts, working each knit/purl pair as k2tog with both colors (all 4 strands) as you BO.

FINISHING

Block pieces lightly to measurements.

Collar

With RS facing, place 152 (200) held neck sts on longer cir needle so there are 51 (67) front sts at each end of needle and 50 (66) back sts in center—75 (99) knit/purl pairs; 1 selvedge st at each side. Join A/D and C/G with RS facing. Work across all sts in solid-color double knitting for 30 (40) rows using A/D on RS and C/G on WS of garment and ending with a WS row—collar measures about 4¾ (6½)" (12 [16.5] cm) high. BO all sts, working each selvedge st as a single st with both colors (all 4 strands), and working each knit/purl pair as k2tog with both colors as you BO.

Join Sleeves

With RS facing and matching color threaded on a tapestry needle, use the mattress st (see Glossary) to sew sleeve seam for RS double-knitting layer only, leaving sides of first block at upper end of sleeve open. Turn sleeve inside out and sew sleeve seam for WS double-knitting layer in the same manner. Rep for second sleeve. Turn one sleeve right side out again—sleeves are now mirror images of each other. Arrange pieces so both right and left sleeves have a block of C/E with an A/D circle at the front armhole corner. Sandwich the BO edge of one sleeve between the unjoined layers of body armhole opening, matching the center of the sleeve with the shoulder join, and easing to fit. With matching color threaded on a tapestry needle, sew RS body layer to RS of sleeve. Turn jacket inside out and sew WS body layer to WS of sleeve, enclosing sleeve BO edge. Sandwich BO edge of body at base of armhole between two layers of block at upper end of sleeve and sew each layer separately in the same manner. Rep for other sleeve.

Weave in loose ends.

PACIFIC

I found the inspiration for this sweater on the beach along Chile's coastline where an old fisherman was wearing a well-loved sweater. The boat was tied up with ropes, which inspired the cables in this sweater.

Finished Size
About 35¾ (39½, 43¾, 48¼)" (91 [100.5, 111, 122.5] cm) bust circumference. Sweater shown photographed flat measures 35¾" (91 cm) in regular length.

Yarn
About 150 (175, 200, 225) grams of a medium color (A) of fingering-weight (#1 Super Fine) yarn and about 175 (200, 225, 250) grams of a light color (B) of the same or a different fingering-weight yarn.

Shown here
Isager Highland (100% wool; 305 yd [279 m]/50 g): topaz (light blue; A), 4 (4, 5, 5) skeins.

Isager Alpaca 2 (50% merino, 50% alpaca; 270 yd [247 m]/50 g): #100 natural (B), 4 (5, 5, 6) skeins.

Needles
Body and sleeves—size U.S. 4 (3.5 mm): 16" and 24" (40 and 60 cm) circular (cir) and set of 4 or 5 double-pointed (dpn). *Facings*—size U.S. 2 (3.0 mm): 16" and 24" (40 and 60 cm) cir and set of 4 or 5 dpn. Adjust needle size if necessary to obtain the correct gauge.

Notions
Marker (m); cable needle (cn); removable markers or waste yarn; tapestry needle; stitch holders; sharp-point sewing needle or sewing machine; contrasting basting thread; matching sewing thread.

Gauge
33 stitches and 34½ rounds = 4" (10 cm) in vertical stripes pattern and colorwork pattern from chart on larger needles, worked in rounds.

STITCH GUIDE

Right-Cross Cable

(worked over 6 sts and 6 rnds, shown on sweater photographed flat)

Rnds 1–5: K1 with A, k4 with B, k1 with A.

Rnd 6: K1 with A, sl 2 sts ono cable needle (cn) and hold in back, k2 with B, k2 from cn with B, k1 with A.

Rep Rnds 1–6 for patt.

Left-Cross Cable

(worked over 6 sts and 4 rnds, shown on sweater worn by model)

Rnds 1–3: K1 with A, k4 with B, k1 with A.

Rnd 4: K1 with A, sl 2 sts onto cable needle (cn) and hold in front, k2 with B, k2 from cn with B, k1 with A.

Rep Rnds 1–4 for patt.

Vertical Stripes

(worked over an odd number of sts)

All rnds: *K1 with B, k1 with A; rep from * to last st, k1 with B.

Rep this rnd for patt.

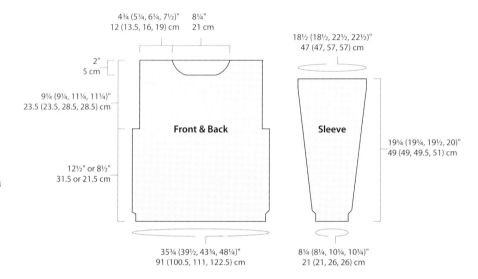

4¾ (5¼, 6¼, 7½)" 8¼"
12 (13.5, 16, 19) cm 21 cm

18½ (18½, 22½, 22½)"
47 (47, 57, 57) cm

2"
5 cm

9¼ (9¼, 11¼, 11¼)"
23.5 (23.5, 28.5, 28.5) cm

Front & Back

Sleeve

19¼ (19¼, 19½, 20)"
49 (49, 49.5, 51) cm

12½" or 8½"
31.5 or 21.5 cm

35¾ (39½, 43¾, 48¼)"
91 (100.5, 111, 122.5) cm

8¼ (8¼, 10¼, 10¼)"
21 (21, 26, 26) cm

NOTES

■ This sweater is worked in stranded two-color knitting (see page 26) with the light color (B) as the dominant color.

■ The body is worked in the round to the shoulder line with steeks for the armhole openings. The front neck shaping is stitched and cut during finishing. The sleeves are worked in the round with facings at the upper edges to cover the raw edges of the steeked armhole openings.

■ The sweater shown photographed flat is worked with right-crossing 6-round cables, but the sweater shown on the model is worked with left-crossing 4-round cables. You may choose either cable for your project, but be sure to use the same cable pattern throughout.

■ Instructions are provided for two different lower body lengths below the armholes, the 12½" (31.5 cm) regular length shown on the sweater photographed flat, and an 8½" (21.5 cm) cropped length shown on the sweater worn by the model. Yarn amounts given are sufficient for making the regular length version.

BODY

With B and longer cir needle in smaller size, CO 246 (272, 302, 332) sts. Place marker (pm) and join for working in rnds. Work in St st (knit every rnd) until piece measures 1" (2.5 cm) from CO. Knit 1 rnd, using the M1 method (see Glossary) to inc 50 (54, 60, 66) sts evenly spaced (about 1 inc for every 5 sts)—296 (326, 362, 398) sts. Purl 1 rnd for turning ridge. Change to longer cir in larger size.

Set-up rnd: *K1 with A, work 6 sts in cable patt of your choice (see Stitch Guide and Notes), [k1 B, k1 A] 0 (2, 2, 2) times, pm, work Rnd 1 (18, 18, 1) of Pacific chart over 135 (135, 153, 171) sts beg and ending where indicated for your size, pm, [k1 with A, k1 with B] 0 (2, 2, 2) times, work 6 sts in cable patt, [k1 with A, work 6 sts in cable patt] 0 (1, 1, 1) time,* pm for left side; rep from * to * for front sts—148 (163, 181, 199) sts each for front and back; rnd beg at start of back sts.

Working sts outside patts in their matching colors, cont in patts as established until 108 chart rnds have been completed for the regular length version, or until 74 chart rnds have been completed for the cropped version, ending with Rnd 6 (23, 23, 6) of chart, and ending last rnd 0 (7, 7, 7) sts before end-of-rnd m—lower body measures 12½" (31.5 cm) from turning ridge for regular length and 8½" (21.5 cm) from turning ridge for cropped length.

Armhole Steeks

Cont in patt, BO 0 (7, 7, 7) sts at end of last rnd, remove end of rnd m, BO first st of next rnd, work to last 0 (7, 7, 7) back sts, BO 0 (7, 7, 7) back sts, remove end-of-rnd m, BO first front st, work in patt to end—294 (310, 346, 382) sts rem; 147 (155, 173, 191) sts each for back and front; 6 cable sts rem on each side of both back and front. Using yarns still attached at end of BO, *pm, use the backward-loop method (see Glossary) to CO 3 steek sts alternating 1 st of each color, pm,* work in established patt to next BO gap; rep from * to * for second steek, work in patt to end—300 (316, 352, 388) sts total; 147 (155, 173, 191) sts each for back and front; 3 steek sts at base of each armhole. On the foll rnds, work the 3 steek sts at each side in a solid color, 1×1 checkerboard patt, or stripes, as you prefer in order to distinguish them from the patt sts. Cont in patt until 62 (62, 79, 79) rnds have been completed from start of armhole steeks for all sizes, ending with Rnd 34 (17, 34, 17) of chart—armholes measure about 7¼ (7¼, 9¼, 9¼)" (18.5 [18.5, 23.5, 23.5] cm). Break yarns.

Neck Shaping

Note: While shaping neck, do not work any partial rhomboid chart shapes; if you think there will not be enough sts or rows to finish a complete rhomboid, work the sts in the established vertical stripe background patt instead.

Mark center 33 front sts with removable markers or waste yarn—57 (61, 70, 79) front sts on each side of marked sts. Slip sts as if to purl (pwise) to m at end of 33 marked center front sts and rejoin yarns at end of marked sts (right neck edge).

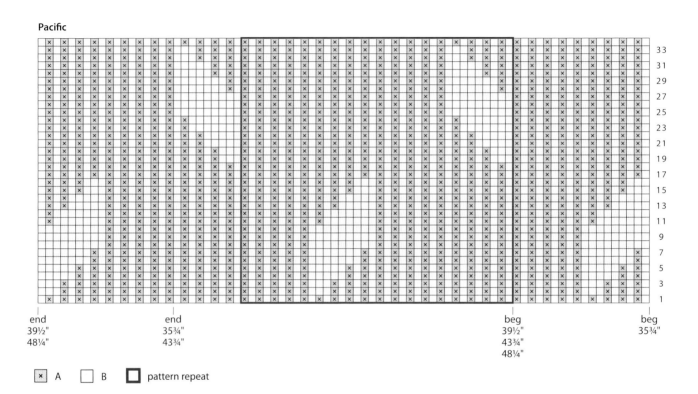

Pacific

33
31
29
27
25
23
21
19
17
15
13
11
9
7
5
3
1

end
39½"
48¼"

end
35¾"
43¾"

beg
39½"
43¾"
48¼"

beg
35¾"

| × | A | | | B | | | | pattern repeat |

Working patts back and forth in rows, shape front neck using short-rows (see page 147) as foll:

Short-row 1: (RS) Work in patt to end of right front sts, across back and steeks, and across left front neck to end at marked center sts (left neck edge), yo with B, turn. Rows now beg and end on each side of front neck.

Short-row 2: (WS) Work in patt to m at right neck edge, yo with B, turn.

Short-rows 3–6: Work in patt to 4 sts before previous turning point, yo with B, turn.

Short-rows 7–16: Work in patt to 2 sts before previous turning point, yo with B, turn—69 sts in shaped center section (not counting yarnovers) after completing Short-row 16; 39 (43, 52, 61) front sts rem on each side of neck shaping.

Short-row 17: Work in patt to end of right front neck, then work in patt across all sts, working yarnovers along left neck edge tog with the sts after them as k2tog with B, and working yarnovers along the right neck edge tog with the sts before them as ssk with B—armholes measure about 9¼ (9¼, 11¼, 11¼)" (23.5 [23.5, 28.5, 28.5] cm).

Place steek sts on holders. Place 39 (43, 52, 61) back and front sts at each side on holders for shoulders, then place rem center 69 back and front sts on holders for neck opening.

SLEEVES

With B and smaller dpn, CO 58 (58, 71, 71) sts. Pm and join for working in rnds. Work in St st until piece measures 1" (2.5 cm) from CO. Knit 1 rnd, using the M1 method to inc 11 (11, 14, 14) sts evenly spaced (about 1 inc for every 5 sts)—69 (69, 85, 85) sts. Purl 1 rnd for turning ridge. Change to larger dpn.

Set-up rnd: K1 with B, work 6 sts in your chosen cable patt, work center 55 (55, 71, 71) sts in vertical stripes patt (see Stitch Guide), work 6 sts in cable patt, k1 with B.

Cont in established patts and *at the same time* inc 1 st at each end of rnd (1 st in from the end) every 4 rnds 28 (22, 0, 5) times, then every 3 rnds 14 (20, 50, 45) times, working new sts in vertical stripes patt and changing to shorter cir in larger size when there are too many sts to fit on dpn—153 (153, 185, 185) sts. Work even in established patts until piece measures 19 (18¼, 18½, 19)" (48.5 [46.5, 47, 48.5] cm) from turning ridge. Change to working back and forth in rows. Work even in patts in rows until piece measures 19¼ (19¼, 19½, 20)" (49 [49, 49.5, 51] cm) from turning ridge, ending with a RS row. Knit 1 WS row with B to mark start of armhole facing, then cont in St st with B for ⅝" (1.5 cm) for facing. BO all sts.

FINISHING

Carefully steam-press pieces to measurements under a damp cloth. **Note:** Sleeve is shown in the round on the schematic even though the final ¼ (1, 1, 1)" (0.6 [2.5, 2.5, 2.5] cm) is worked in rows below the facing turning ridge; armhole facings are not shown on schematic.

Armhole Steeks

Baste a line of contrasting thread along the center of each 3-st steek. With sewing machine or by hand, sew a line of small straight stitches one stitch away on each side of the basting line. Sew over the same two lines of stitching again. Carefully cut open each armhole along the basting line.

Neckband

Join 39 (43, 52, 61) shoulder sts of back and front using the three-needle bind-off method (see Glossary)—69 held sts rem each at center back and front. Place 138 live sts of neck opening on shorter cir needle in larger size with RS facing so that front sts will be worked first. Join A and B to beg of neck sts at left shoulder join. Rm and join for working in rnds as foll:

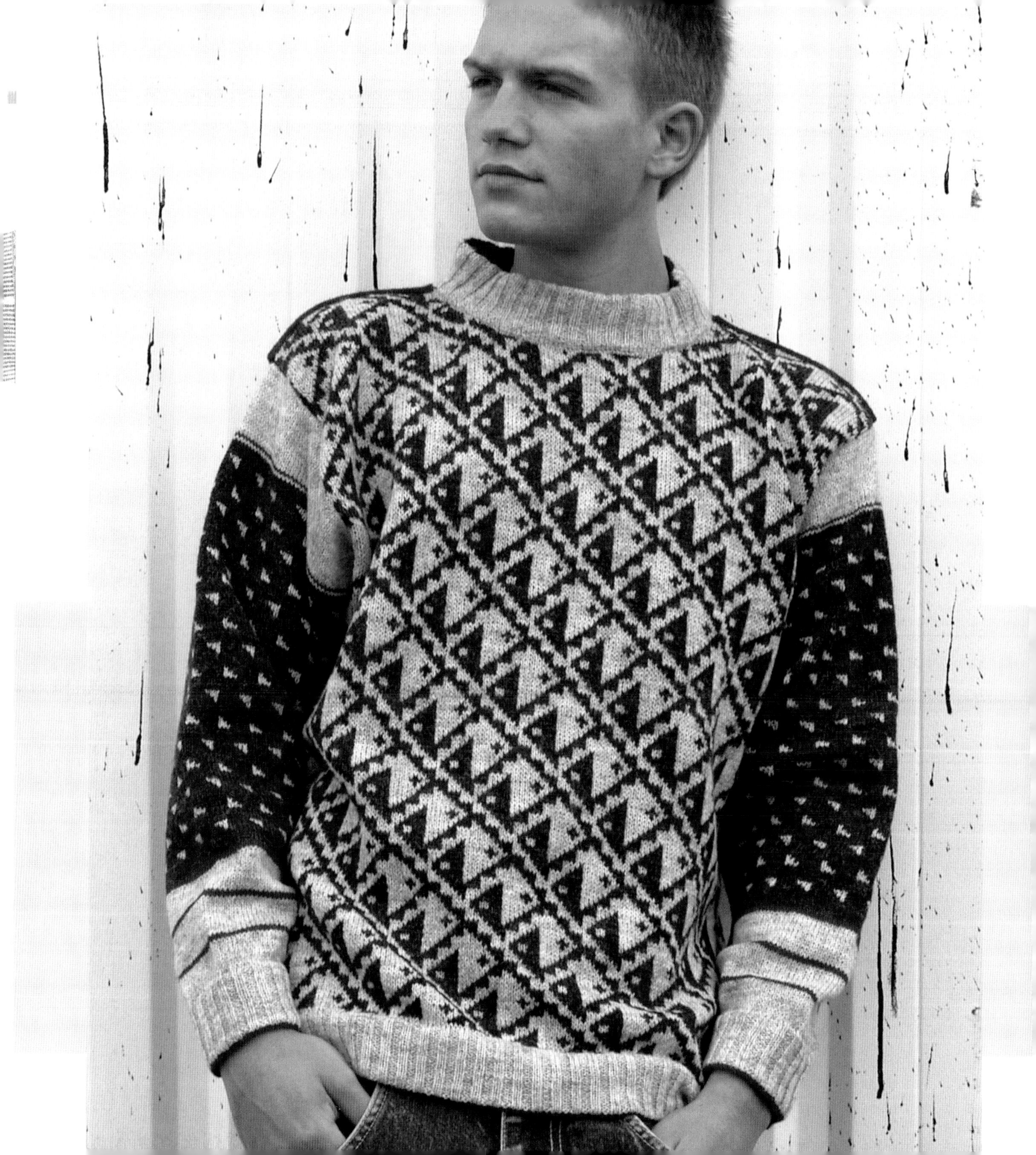

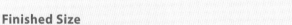

FISH FANTASY

I found the motif for this sweater
on a woven carpet on display
in a museum in Lima, Peru.

Finished Size
About 37½ (39½, 43¾, 45¾)" (95 [100.5, 111, 116] cm) bust/chest
circumference. Sweater shown photographed flat measures 43¾"
(111 cm) in tunic length.

Yarn
About 225 (250, 275, 300) grams of a light color (A), 150 (175, 200, 225)
grams of a dark color (B), and 40 (50, 60, 70) grams of an accent color
(C) of fingering-weight (#1 Super Fine) yarn.

Shown here
For sweater on model: Isager Alpaca 2 (50% merino, 50% alpaca;
270 yd [247 m]/40 g): #2105 light gray heather (A), 5 (5, 6, 6) skeins; #025
coral (C), 1 (1, 2, 2) skein(s).

Isager Highland (100% wool; 305 yd [279 m]/50 g): Oxford (B),
3 (4, 4, 5) skeins.

For sweater photographed flat: Isager Alpaca 2 (50% merino, 50%
alpaca; 270 yd [247 m]/40 g). #100 natural (A), 5 (5, 6, 6) skeins; #011
steel blue, 3 (4, 4, 5) skeins; and #013 dusty plum (C), 1 (1, 2, 2) skein(s).

Needles
Body and sleeves—size U.S. 2 (3.0 mm): 16" and 24" (40 and
60 cm) circular (cir) and set of 4 or 5 double-pointed (dpn).
Facings and ribbing—size U.S. 1 (2.5 mm): 16" and 24" (40
and 60 cm) cir and set of 4 or 5 dpn. Adjust needle size if
necessary to obtain the correct gauge.

Notions
Markers (m); stitch holders; tapestry needle; sharp-point
sewing needle or sewing machine; contrasting basting
thread; matching sewing thread.

Gauge
35 stitches and 39 rounds = 4" (10 cm) in stockinette-stitch
colorwork patterns from charts on larger needles, worked in
rounds; 31 stitches and 39 rounds = 4" (10 cm) in solid-color
stockinette on larger needle, worked in rounds.

STITCH GUIDE

K2, P2 Rib

(multiple of 4 sts)

All rnds: P1, *k2, p2; rep from * to last 3 sts, k2, p1.

Rep this rnd for patt.

Vertical Stripes

(worked over an odd number of sts)

All rnds: *K1 with A, k1 with B; rep from * to last st, k1 with A.

Rep this rnd for patt.

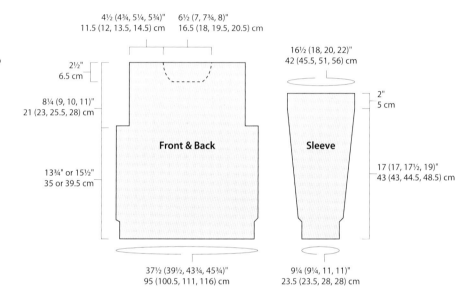

4½ (4¾, 5¼, 5¾)"
11.5 (12, 13.5, 14.5) cm

6½ (7, 7¾, 8)"
16.5 (18, 19.5, 20.5) cm

16½ (18, 20, 22)"
42 (45.5, 51, 56) cm

2½"
6.5 cm

8¼ (9, 10, 11)"
21 (23, 25.5, 28) cm

2"
5 cm

Front & Back

Sleeve

13¾" or 15½"
35 or 39.5 cm

17 (17, 17½, 19)"
43 (43, 44.5, 48.5) cm

37½ (39½, 43¾, 45¾)"
95 (100.5, 111, 116) cm

9¼ (9¼, 11, 11)"
23.5 (23.5, 28, 28) cm

NOTES

■ This sweater is worked in stranded two-color knitting (see page 26).

■ The body is worked in the round to the shoulder line, with steeks for the armhole openings. The front neck shaping is stitched and cut during finishing. The sleeves are worked in the round with facings at the upper edges to cover the raw edges of the steeked armhole openings.

■ Instructions are provided for two different lower body lengths below the armholes; the 13¾" (35 cm) regular length shown on the sweater worn by the model and a 15½" (39.5 cm) tunic length shown on the sweater photographed flat. Yarn amounts given are sufficient for making the longer tunic version.

BODY

With C and longer cir needle in smaller size, CO 276 (288, 320, 336) sts. Place marker (pm) and join for working in rnds. Work in St st (knit every rnd) until piece measures 2¼" (5.5 cm) from CO. Purl 1 rnd for turning ridge, then knit 1 more rnd. Change to A and knit 1 rnd. Work in k2, p2 rib (see Stitch Guide) until piece measures 2¼" (5.5 cm) from turning ridge. Change to longer cir needle in larger size. Knit 1 rnd, inc 52 (58, 62, 64) sts evenly spaced—328 (346, 382, 400) sts.

Set-up rnd: *K1 with B, work 15 sts in vertical stripes patt (see Stitch Guide), pm, establish patt from Rnd 1 of Fantasy Body chart over next 133 (142, 160, 169) sts by working 27-st rep 4 (5, 5, 6) times, then work 25 (7, 25, 7) sts after patt rep box to end where indicated for your size, pm, work 15 sts in vertical stripes patt,* pm for left side; rep from * to * for front sts—164 (173, 191, 200) sts each for front and back; rnd beg at start of back sts.

Cont in patts as established until piece measures from turning ridge 13¾" (35 cm) for regular length body, or 15½" (39.5 cm) for tunic length, ending last rnd 14 sts before end-of-rnd m.

Armhole Steeks

Cont in patt, BO last 14 sts of previous rnd and first 15 sts of next rnd for right armhole removing end-of-rnd m as you come to it (1 color A stripe st rem on needle after last BO), work to end of back chart patt, k1 with A, BO next 29 sts for left armhole removing left side m as you come to it, work to end of front

A woven carpet inspired the pattern of Fish Fantasy.

chart patt, k1 with A—135 (144, 162, 171) sts each for back and front; rem sts for both back and front should be 133 (142, 160, 169) chart sts with 1 color A st at each side.

Next rnd: Using yarns still attached at end of BO, *pm, use the backward-loop method (see Glossary) to CO 3 steek sts alternating 1 st of each color, pm,* work in established patt to next BO gap; rep from * to * for second steek, work in patt to end—276 (294, 330, 348) sts total; 135 (144, 162, 171) sts each for back and front; 3 steek sts at base of each armhole.

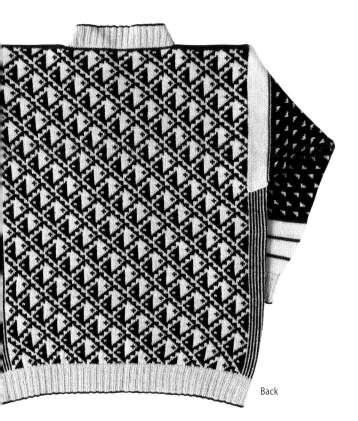

Back

On the foll rnds, work the 3 steek sts at each side in a solid color, 1×1 checkerboard patt, or stripes, as you prefer in order to distinguish them from the patt sts.

Regular Length Only
Cont in patt until 189 (199, 208, 216) chart rnds have been completed, ending with Rnd 27 (10, 19, 27) of chart.

Tunic Length Only
Cont in patt until 208 (216, 226, 235) chart rnds have been completed, ending with Rnd 19 (27, 10, 19) of chart.

Both Lengths
Change to C and knit 2 rnds—armholes measure about 8¼ (9, 10, 11)" (21 [23, 25.5, 28] cm). Place steek sts on holders. Place 39 (41, 47, 50) back and front sts at each side on holders for shoulders, then place rem center 57 (62, 68, 71) back and front sts on holders for neck opening.

SLEEVES
With C and smaller dpn, CO 60 (60, 68, 68) sts. Pm and join for working in rnds. Work in St st until piece measures 2¼" (5.5 cm) from CO. Purl 1 rnd for turning ridge, then knit 1 more rnd. Change to A and knit 1 rnd. Work in k2, p2 rib until piece measures 2¼" (5.5 cm) from turning ridge. Change to larger dpn. Knit 1 rnd, inc 12 (12, 18, 18) sts evenly spaced—72 (72, 86, 86) sts.

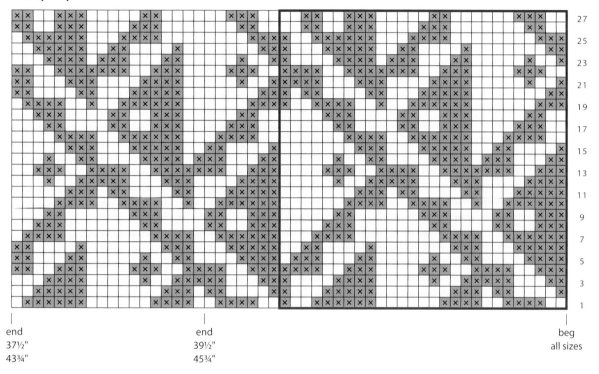

Fantasy Body

27
25
23
21
19
17
15
13
11
9
7
5
3
1

end
37½"
43¾"

end
39½"
45¾"

beg
all sizes

Next 41 rnds: Work 11 rnds A, 2 rnds C, [12 rnds A, 2 rnds C] 2 times and *at the same time* inc 1 st at each end of rnd (1 st in from end-of-rnd m) every 8 rnds 5 times—82 (82, 96, 96) sts.

With B, knit 1 rnd, inc 10 (10, 12, 12) sts evenly spaced—92 (92, 108, 108) sts; piece measures about 6¾" (17 cm) from turning ridge. Work Rnd 1 of Fantasy Sleeve chart. Cont in patt until 100 (100, 106, 120) chart rnds total have been completed, ending with Rnd 2 (2, 8, 8) of chart and *at the same time* inc 1 st at each end of rnd every 5 rnds 18 (3, 9, 0) times,

Fantasy Sleeve

13
11
9
7
5
3
1

☐ A

☒ B

☐ pattern repeat

then every 4 rnds 0 (21, 15, 25) times, then every 3 rnds 0 (0, 0, 6) times, working new sts into chart patt, and changing to shorter cir in larger size when there are too many sts to fit on dpn—128 (140, 156, 170) sts; piece measures about 17 (17, 17½, 19)" (43 [43, 44.5, 48.5] cm) from turning ridge. Change to working back and forth in rows in St st.

Next 3 rows: Knit 1 RS row with B, purl 1 WS row with A, knit 1 RS row with C.

Cont in St st with A for 1¾" (4.5 cm) or to desired total length, ending with a RS row—piece measures about 19 (19, 19½, 21)" (48.5 [48.5, 49.5, 53.5] cm) from turning ridge. Knit 1 WS row to mark start of armhole facing, then cont in St st for ⅝" (1.5 cm) more for facing. BO all sts.

FINISHING

Carefully steam-press pieces to measurements under a damp cloth. **Note:** Sleeve is shown in the round on the schematic even though the final 2" (5 cm) is worked in rows; armhole facings are not shown on schematic.

Armhole Steeks

Baste a line of contrasting thread along the center of each 3-st steek. With sewing machine or by hand, sew a line of small straight stitches one stitch away on each side of the basting line. Sew over the same two lines of stitching again. Carefully cut open each armhole along the basting line.

Front Neck

Join 39 (41, 47, 50) shoulder sts of back and front using the three-needle bind-off method (see Glossary)— 57 (62, 68, 71) held sts rem at center back and front. Measure down 2½" (6.5 cm) from exact center of front sts on holder. Baste the outline of a curved neck opening as shown by dotted line on schematic, beg and ending the curve at the edges of the live front neck sts. Sew two lines of small straight stitches along the basting line. Cut out the neck shaping about ¼" (6 mm) inside the basting line to leave a small seam allowance.

Neckband

With A, shorter cir needle in smaller size, and RS facing, knit across 57 (62, 68, 71) held back neck sts, then pick up and knit 67 (70, 72, 77) sts along cut front neck edge, picking up below the sewing line so neckline stitching does not show on RS of garment—124 (132, 140, 148) sts. Pm and join for working in rnds. Work in k2, p2 rib until piece measures 1½" (3.8 cm) from pick-up rnd. Change to C and knit 1 rnd, then purl 1 rnd for neckband turning ridge. Work even in St st with C until piece measures 1¾" (4.5 cm) from turning ridge. BO all sts loosely. Fold neckband facing to WS along turning ridge and sew invisibly in place so that it covers the cut front neck edge.

Sew sleeves into armholes, sewing between the first patt st and outermost steek st on the body and sewing just below the purled ridge at the top of the sleeve so purled sleeve sts do not show on RS of garment. Sew facings at tops of sleeves invisibly on WS to conceal cut edges of steeks. Sew short selvedges at tops of sleeves to BO sts at base of armholes.

Weave in loose ends.

INTARSIA KNITTING

Intarsia is a method of working isolated areas of color. Separate balls of yarn are used for each section, or block, of color. The most important thing to remember when knitting intarsia is that the yarns need to be twisted around each other at the color changes. Otherwise, there will be gaps (holes) between the different colors of knitting.

Practice Intarsia Knitting

To practice intarsia knitting, you will needles and one ball each of a dark- and light-colored yarn. With the dark yarn, cast on 4 stitches. With the light yarn, cast on 4 more stitches onto the same needle (Figure 1). Turn the work around to work the first wrong-side row. Work in stockinette stitch as follows:

Wrong-Side (Purl) Rows

With the light yarn, purl the 4 light stitches, then drop the light yarn to front (purl side) of the work. Pick up the dark yarn from underneath the light yarn (Figure 2), then use it to purl the 4 dark stitches.

Right-Side (Knit) Rows

With the dark yarn, knit the 4 dark stitches, then drop the dark yarn to the back (purl side) of the work. Pick up the light yarn over the dark yarn (Figure 3), then knit the next 4 stitches with the light yarn.

Repeat these two rows, always dropping the old color to the wrong (purl) side of the work and always picking up the new color from under the old. Pull gently on the new color before knitting the first stitch to close the gap between the two colors.

If a pattern calls for many blocks of color in the same row, wind a separate butterfly of yarn for each section to prevent the yarns from tangling on each other. To make a butterfly, wind the yarn into a figure-eight around your thumb and little finger the desired number of times. To finish, wind the yarn around the center of the bundle a couple of times, then secure the tail on one of these center wraps (Figure 4). Pull the working end from the center (shown with an arrow) as needed.

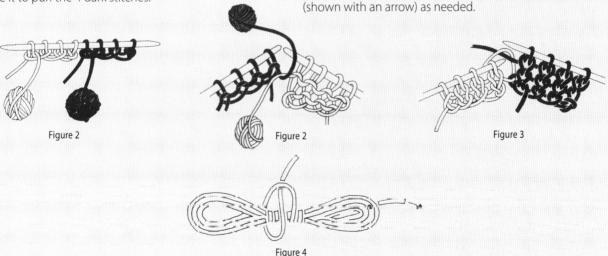

Figure 2

Figure 2

Figure 3

Figure 4

INCA CHILD

When I was two years old, my mother's aunt Else gave me a colorful hat from Peru. The bright colors and lovely border of dancing boys and girls has always made me happy, and I've included them in this sweater.

Finished Size

Sweater: About 17½ (20½, 22, 25, 28, 29½)" (44.5 [52, 56, 63.5, 71, 75] cm) chest circumference, to fit children's sizes 6 months (1, 2, 4, 6, 8) years. Sweater shown photographed flat measures 25" (63.5 cm).

Cap: About 17½ (19)" (44.5 [48.5] cm) head circumference. Cap shown on page 62 measures 17½" (44.5 cm).

Yarn

Sweater: About 50 (60, 70, 80, 90, 110) grams of main color (A), 40 (50, 60, 70, 80, 90) grams of second color (B), 15 (20, 25, 30, 35, 40) grams each of two contrasting colors (C6 and C7), and small amounts of eight other contrasting colors (C1, C2, C3, C4, C5, C8, C9, and C10) of fingering-weight (#1 Super Fine) yarn.

Cap: About 20 grams of main color (A), 15 grams of second color (B) and small amounts of ten contrasting colors (C1, C2, C3, C4, C5, C6, C7, C8, C9, and C10) of fingering-weight (#1 Super Fine) yarn.

Shown here

Sweater: Isager Alpaca 2 (50% merino, 50% alpaca; 270 yd [247 m]/50 g): bright red (A; discontinued), 1 (2, 2, 2, 2, 3) skein(s); #022 rose (B), 1 (1, 2, 2, 2, 2) skein(s); #019 very light blue (C1), medium blue (C2; discontinued), #020 teal (C3), aqua (C4; discontinued); #16 chartreuse (C5), lime (C6; discontinued), bottle green (C7; discontinued), cerise (C8; discontinued), #014 orange (C9), and light pink (C10; discontinued), 1 skein each. **Note:** Substitute the colors of your choice for the discontinued colors.

Cap: Same yarn and colors as sweater, 1 skein each of all twelve colors.

Needles

Sweater body and sleeves—size U.S. 2 (3.0 mm): 16" and 24" (40 and 60 cm) circular and set of 4 or 5 double-pointed (dpn). *Sweater facings and neckband*—size U.S. 1 (2.5 mm): 16" and 24" (40 and 60 cm) cir and set of 4 or 5 dpn. Adjust needle size if necessary to obtain the correct gauge.

Cap—Size U.S. 3 (3.25 mm) double-pointed (dpn). *Earflaps*—size U.S. 1 to 2 (2.5 to 2.75 mm) set of 2 dpn. Adjust needle size if necessary to obtain the correct gauge.

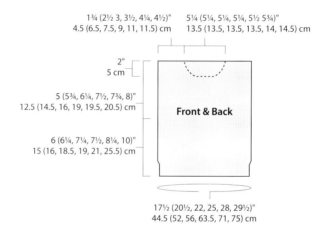

Notions

Markers (m); stitch holders; tapestry needle; sharp-point sewing needle or sewing machine (for sweater steeks); contrasting basting thread and matching sewing thread (for sweater steeks); size C/2 (3 mm) crochet hook (for cap edging).

Gauge

Sweater: 33 stitches and 46 rounds = 4" (10 cm) in stockinette stitch on larger needles, worked in rounds.

Cap: 29 stitches and 41 rounds = 4" (10 cm) in stockinette stitch on larger needles, worked in rounds.

STITCH GUIDE

Vertical Stripes

(worked over an odd number of sts)

All rnds: *K1 with C7, k1 with C6; rep from * to last st, k1 with C7.

Rep this rnd for patt.

Vertical Stripes

(worked over an even number of sts)

All rnds: *K1 with C7, k1 with C6; rep from *.

Rep this rnd for patt.

1¾ (2½ 3, 3½, 4¼, 4½)"
4.5 (6.5, 7.5, 9, 11, 11.5) cm

5¼ (5¼, 5¼, 5¼, 5½ 5¾)"
13.5 (13.5, 13.5, 13.5, 14, 14.5) cm

10¼ (11½, 12½, 14, 15¼, 16)"
26 (29, 31.5, 35.5, 38.5, 40.5) cm

2"
5 cm

5 (5¾, 6¼, 7½, 7¾, 8)"
12.5 (14.5, 16, 19, 19.5, 20.5) cm

Front & Back

6 (6¼, 7¼, 7½, 8¼, 10)"
15 (16, 18.5, 19, 21, 25.5) cm

17½ (20½, 22, 25, 28, 29½)"
44.5 (52, 56, 63.5, 71, 75) cm

Sleeve

8½ (9½, 10½, 12, 13, 13½)"
21.5 (24, 26.5, 30.5, 33, 34.5) cm

5½ (6, 6½, 6½, 7, 7)"
14 (15, 16.5, 16.5, 18, 18) cm

NOTES

- The sweater and cap are worked partially in stranded two-color knitting (see page 26).

- The sweater body is worked in the round to the shoulder line with steeks for the armhole openings. The front neck shaping is sewn and cut during finishing. The sleeves are worked in the round with facings at the upper edges to cover the raw edges of the steeked armhole openings.

- The cap earflaps are worked separately, back and forth in rows. For the start of the cap brim, stitches are picked up along the upper edges of the earflaps and also cast-on between the earflaps for the back and front of the head, then joined for working in rounds to the top.

BODY

With A and longer cir needle in smaller size, CO 140 (160, 180, 200, 220, 240) sts. Place marker (pm) and join for working in rnds; rnd beg at start of back sts. Work in St st (knit all sts every rnd) until piece measures 1½" (3.8 cm) from CO. Change to longer cir needle in larger size. Purl 1 rnd for turning ridge, then knit 1 more rnd.

Set-up rnd: *Work 70 (80, 90, 100, 110, 120) sts in patt from Rnd 1 of Dancers chart, beg and ending where indicated for your size,* pm for left side, rep from * to * once more for front sts—70 (80, 90, 100, 110, 120) sts each for back and front.

Work in established patt until Rnd 16 of chart has been completed. With C5, knit 2 rnds, inc 2 (4, 0, 2, 4, 0) sts evenly spaced on both back and front in second rnd—144 (168, 180, 204, 228, 240) sts total; 72 (84, 90, 102, 114, 120) sts each for back and front; piece measures about 1½" (3.8 cm) from turning ridge. Change to A, and work even in St st until piece measures about 4¼ (4½, 5¼, 5¾, 6¼, 7)" (11 [11.5, 13.5, 14.5, 16, 18] cm) from turning ridge. Work Rnds 1–4 of Sweater Wave chart using A for blank squares and C1 for X symbols. Knit 2 rnds each of C4, C2, and C3. Change to B and work even in St st until piece measures 6 (6¼, 7¼, 7½, 8¼, 10)" (15 [16, 18.5, 19, 21, 25.5] cm) from turning ridge.

Armhole Steeks

CO 3 sts for right armhole steek, pm, knit to end of back sts, slip side m, CO 3 sts for left armhole steek,

This hat inspired the colors and pattern of Inca Child.

pm, knit to end of front sts—150 (174, 186, 210, 234, 246) sts total; 72 (84, 90, 102, 114, 120) sts each for back and front; 3 steek sts at each armhole. Cont in St st with B until armholes measure 2 (2¼, 2¾, 3½, 3¾, 3¾)" (5 [5.5, 7, 8.5, 9.5, 9.5] cm). **Note:** On the foll multicolor rnds, work the 3 steek sts at each side in a solid color, 1×1 checkerboard patt, or stripes, as you prefer in order to distinguish them from the patt sts.

Next rnd: *Work 3 steek sts, work 72 (84, 90, 102, 114, 120) sts in patt from Rnd 1 of Sweater Wave chart using B for blank squares and C5 for X symbols,* sl m, rep from * to * once more for front sts.

Work Rnds 2–4 of chart and steeks as established. Knit 2 rnds each of C10, C8, and C9, inc 1 st each on back and front in last rnd—152 (176, 188, 212, 236,

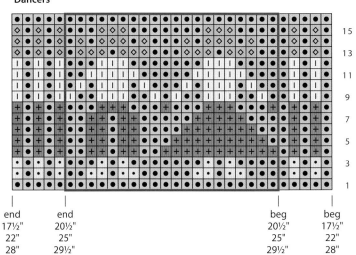

Cap Wave

Sweater Wave

Dancers

end	end		beg	beg
17½"	20½"		20½"	17½"
22"	25"		25"	22"
28"	29½"		29½"	28"

☐ A or B (see instructions)   ▯ C5

☒ C1 or C5 (see instructions)   ● C7

▦ A   ◇ C8

· C1   ☐ pattern repeat

248) sts total; 73 (85, 91, 103, 115, 121) sts each for back and front; 3 steek sts at each armhole.

Next rnd: *Work 3 steek sts, work 73 (85, 91, 103, 115, 121) sts in vertical stripes patt (see Stitch Guide),* sl m, rep from * to * once more for front sts.

Cont in established patt until armholes measure 5 (5¾, 6¼, 7½, 7¾, 8)" (12.5 [14.5, 16, 19, 19.5, 20.5] cm). Place steek sts on holders. Place 15 (21, 24, 30, 35, 37) back and front sts at each side on holders for shoulders, then place rem center 43 (43, 43, 43, 45, 47) back and front sts on holders for neck opening.

SLEEVES

With A and smaller dpn, CO 46 (50, 54, 54, 58, 58) sts. Pm and join for working in rnds. Work in St st until piece measures 1 (1¼, 1¼, 1½, 1½, 2)" (2.5 [3.2, 3.2, 3.8, 3.8, 5] cm) from CO. Purl 1 rnd for turning ridge, then knit 1 more rnd. Change to larger dpn. Work in vertical stripes patt until piece measures 1 (1¼, 1¼, 1½, 1½, 2)" (2.5 [3.2, 3.2, 3.8, 3.8, 5] cm) from turning ridge. Change to A and knit 1 rnd, inc 12 (14, 14, 14, 16, 16) sts evenly spaced—58 (64, 68, 68, 74, 74) sts. Cont in St st with A and *at the same time* inc 1 st at each end of rnd (1 st in from the m) every 4 rnds 4 (10, 11, 7, 0, 14) times, then every 5 rnds 3 (0, 0, 4, 11, 0) times, changing to shorter cir needle in larger size when there are too many sts to fit on dpn—72 (84, 90, 90, 96, 102) sts; piece measures

about 3¾ (4¾, 5¼, 5¾, 6¼, 7)" (9.5 [12, 13.5, 14.5, 16, 18] cm) from turning ridge. Work Rnds 1–4 of Sweater Wave chart using A for blank squares and C5 for X symbols. Knit 2 rnds each of C10, C8, and C9 and *at the same time* inc 1 st at each end of rnd on the first rnd—74 (86, 92, 92, 98, 104) sts. Change to B. Cont in St st, inc 1 st at each end of rnd every 5 (5, 5, 4, 3, 3) rnds 5 (5, 5, 11, 14, 14) times—84 (96, 102, 114, 126, 132) sts. Work even in St st with B until piece measures about 7½ (8½, 9½, 11, 12, 12½)" (19 [21.5, 24, 28, 30.5, 31.5] cm) from turning ridge, or 1" (2.5 cm) less than desired length. Work Rnds 1–4 of Sweater Wave chart using B for blank squares and C1 for X symbols. Knit 2 rnds each of C4, C2, and C3—piece measures about 8½ (9½, 10½, 12, 13, 13½)" (21.5 [24, 26.5, 30.5, 33, 34.5] cm) from turning ridge. With C3, purl 1 rnd, then work in St st for ⅜ (⅜, ⅜, ⅝, ⅝, ⅝)" (1 [1, 1, 1.5, 1.5, 1.5] cm) for armhole facing. BO all sts.

FINISHING

Carefully steam-press pieces to measurements under a damp cloth. **Note:** Armhole facings are not shown on schematic.

Steeks

Baste a line of contrasting thread along the center of each 3-st steek. With sewing machine or by hand, sew a line of small straight stitches one stitch away on each side of the basting line. Sew over the same two lines of stitching again.

Back

Carefully cut open each armhole along the basting line.

Front Neck

Join 15 (21, 24, 30, 35, 37) shoulder sts of back and front using the three-needle bind-off method (see Glossary)—43 (43, 43, 43, 45, 47) held sts rem at center back and front. Measure down 2" (5 cm) from exact center of front sts on holder. Baste the outline of a curved neck opening as shown by dotted line on schematic, beg and ending the curve at the edges of the live front neck sts. Sew two lines of small straight stitches along the basting line. Cut out the neck shaping about ¼" (6 mm) inside the basting line to leave a small seam allowance.

Neckband

Using shorter cir needle in smaller size, C5, and RS facing, knit across 43 (43, 43, 43, 45, 47) held back neck sts, then pick up and knit 59 (59, 59, 59, 61, 63) sts along front neck, picking up below the sewing line so neckline stitching does not show on RS of garment—102 (102, 102, 102, 106, 110) sts total. Pm and join for working in rnds. With C5, knit 1 rnd, inc 3 (inc 3, inc 3, inc 3, dec 1, dec 5) sts evenly spaced—105 sts for all sizes. With C5, purl 1 rnd. The neckband is worked in rows of garter st blocks, joining the garter neckband sts to the live picked-up sts around the neck opening at the end of each RS row. Change to C6, and with RS facing use the knitted method (see Glossary) to CO 15 sts onto left needle tip.

Next row: (RS) With C6, sl 1 knitwise with yarn in back (kwise wyb), k13, k2tog (last neckband st tog with 1 neck opening st), turn—1 neckband st joined.

Next row: (WS) Sl 1 kwise wyb, knit to end.

Rep the last 2 rows for neckband and *at the same time* change colors as foll or as desired: Work 12 more rows with C6, then work 14 rows each with C10, C3, C1, C5, C7, C9, C3, C6, C10, C3, C1, C5, C9, and C2—15 garter blocks completed of 14 rows and 7 garter ridges each; all picked-up sts have been joined. With RS facing, slip a dpn into the 15 loops at CO end of border; these loops are just picked up and placed on the needle, not picked up and knitted. Hold dpns with live neckband sts and picked-up sts tog with RS touching and use the three-needle bind-off method to join the CO and BO ends of neckband. Fold neckband in half and sew invisibly in place so that it covers the cut front neck edge.

Sew sleeves into armholes, sewing between the first patt st and outermost steek st on the body, and sewing just below the purled ridge at the top of the sleeve so purled sleeve sts do not show on RS of garment. Sew facings at tops of sleeves invisibly on WS to conceal cut edges of steeks. Turn lower border and cuff facings to WS along turning ridges and use A threaded on a tapestry needle to sew facings in place on WS. Weave in loose ends.

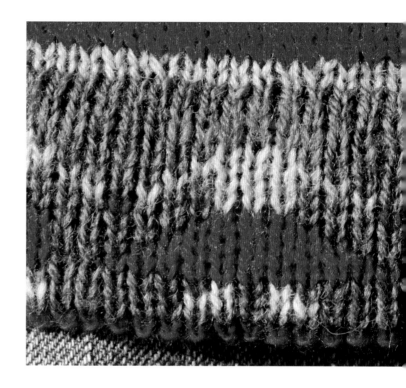

Steam seams, facings, and neckband again carefully, if desired.

CAP

Earflap (make 2)

With C3 and smaller dpn, CO 28 sts, leaving a long tail for seaming later.

Set-up row: (WS) K13, place marker (pm), k2, pm, k13.

Inc row: (RS) Knit to m, use the M1 method (see

Glossary) to inc 1 st, slip marker (sl m), k2, sl m, M1, knit to end—2 sts inc'd.

Knit 1 WS row. Rep the last 2 rows 10 more times, working colors in the foll order: 2 more rows C3, 2 rows C2, 2 rows C4, 2 rows C1, 2 rows C10, 2 rows C8, 2 rows C9, 2 rows A, 4 rows B—50 sts; 22 rows and 11 garter ridges completed. Break yarn.

Earflap Edging

The edging is worked in rows of garter-st blocks, joining the garter edging sts to the live sts of the earflap at end of each RS row. Change to C7, and, with RS facing, use the knitted method (see Glossary) to CO 7 sts onto left needle.

Next row: (RS) With C7, k6, k2tog (last edging st tog with 1 earflap st), turn—1 earflap st joined.

Next row: (WS) Knit.

Rep the last 2 rows for edging and *at the same time* change colors as foll: Work 6 more rows with C7, then work 8 rows each with A, C5, C2, C10, and C3—6 color blocks completed of 8 rows and 4 garter ridges each. With C1, rep the last 2 rows once more—25 unjoined earflap sts rem. Work short-rows (see page 147) to turn corner at bottom of earflap using C1 as foll:

Short-row 1: (RS) K3, turn.

Short-row 2: (WS) Yo, k3, turn.

Short-row 3: K3, work yo tog with st after it as ssk, k2, k2tog (last edging st tog with 1 earflap st).

Next row: (WS) Knit to end—3 garter ridges with C1 at outer edge (beg of RS rows); 24 unjoined earflap sts rem.

Cont as established work 8 rows each with C3, C10, C2, C5, A, and C7—6 color blocks completed after center-short-rowed block; all earflap sts have been joined. BO all sts. Fold piece to bring two halves of earflap CO row tog and curve earflap into a U shape as shown. With long CO tail threaded on tapestry needle, sew halves of CO edge tog. Make a second earflap with edging in the same manner.

Brim

With A and larger dpn, CO 9 (11) sts for one-half of back, with RS facing pick up and knit 36 sts along straight selvedge at top of left earflap, CO 36 (44) sts for front, pick up and knit 36 sts along straight selvedge of right earflap, CO 9 (11) sts for other half of back—126 (138) sts total. Pm and join for working in rnds; rnd beg at center back. With A, knit 4 rnds. Work Rnds 1–4 of Cap Wave chart using A for blank squares and C1 for X symbols. Knit 2 rnds each of C4, C2, and C3. Change to B and work in St st for 2" (5 cm)—piece measures about 3¼" (8.5 cm) from brim CO. Work Rnds 1–4 of Cap Wave chart using B for blank squares and C5 for X symbols. Knit 2 rnds each of C10, C8, and C6. Change to A and knit 1 rnd, placing m after every 21 (23) sts—6

marked sections; piece measures about 4¼" (11 cm) from brim CO.

Shape Top

Dec rnd: *Knit to last 6 sts of marked section, ssk, k2, k2tog, slip marker (sl m); rep from * to end—12 sts dec'd, 2 sts from each section. Knit 5 rnds with A. Cont in St st with A, rep the shaping of the last 6 rnds 6 (7) more times, then work dec rnd once more—30 sts rem for both sizes, 5 sts in each section.

Knit 5 rnds.

Next rnd: *Ssk, k1, k2tog; rep from *—18 sts rem; 3 sts in each section.

Next rnd: *K2tog; rep from *—9 sts rem; piece measures about 9 (9¾)" (23 [25] cm) from brim CO.

Cut yarn, leaving a long tail. Thread tail on tapestry needle, run tail through all sts, and pull snugly to close top of cap.

Finishing

With C9, make a 2" (5 cm) tassel (see Glossary), and attach tassel to top of hat as shown. Using crochet hook, join A to center back brim CO edge. With RS facing, work 1 rnd of single crochet (see Glossary) across half of back edge to right earflap, around right earflap, across front brim CO sts, around left earflap, and across rem half of back to center, being careful to work loosely to edge of applica flat without puckering. Join with a slip stitch in first single crochet, then fasten off last st. Weave in loose ends.

STARS

The little star pattern I found on a
Peruvian cap is also recognizable in
Scandinavia. It is most often used on
Norwegian sweaters, but in the old days
in Denmark it was used as an embossed
pattern of knit and purl stitches.

Finished Size
About 34¾ (39¾, 44¾, 49½)" (88.5 [101, 113.5, 125.5] cm) bust
circumference. Sweater shown photographed flat measures
44¾" (113.5 cm).

Yarn
About 150 (175, 200, 250) grams of a light color (A), 125 (150,
175, 225) grams of a dark color (B), and about 10 to 20 grams each
of 6 accent colors (C, D, E, F, G, H) of fingering-weight (#1 Super
Fine) yarn.

Shown here
Isager Alpaca 2 (50% merino, 50% alpaca; 270 yd [247 m]/50 g):
#100 natural (A), 3 (4, 4, 5) skeins; #402 charcoal (B), 3 (3, 4, 5) skeins;
#012 grayed olive (C), #025 coral (D), #020 teal (E), #022 rose (F),
#023 blue (G), and #014 orange (H), 1 skein each.

Needles
Body and sleeves—size U.S. 4 (3.5 mm): 16" and 24" (40 and 60 cm)
circular (cir) and set of 4 or 5 double-pointed (dpn). *Lower border,
cuffs, and neckband*—size U.S. 2 (3 mm): 16" (40 cm) cir and set of 4
or 5 dpn. Adjust needle size if necessary to obtain the correct gauge.

Notions
Markers (m); removable markers or waste yarn; tapestry needle;
sharp-point sewing needle or sewing machine; contrasting basting
thread; matching sewing thread.

Gauge
24 stitches and 33 rounds = 4" (10 cm) in stockinette-stitch colorwork
patterns from chart on larger needle, worked in rounds; 28 stitches
and 50 rounds = 4" (10 cm) in garter stitch on smaller needles.

STARS

59

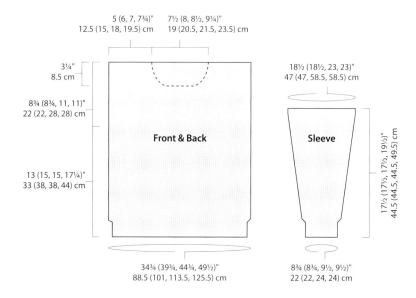

5 (6, 7, 7¾)"
12.5 (15, 18, 19.5) cm

7½ (8, 8½, 9¼)"
19 (20.5, 21.5, 23.5) cm

3¼"
8.5 cm

8¾ (8¾, 11, 11)"
22 (22, 28, 28) cm

Front & Back

13 (15, 15, 17¼)"
33 (38, 38, 44) cm

34¾ (39¾, 44¾, 49½)"
88.5 (101, 113.5, 125.5) cm

18½ (18½, 23, 23)"
47 (47, 58.5, 58.5) cm

Sleeve

17½ (17½, 17½, 19½)"
44.5 (44.5, 44.5, 49.5) cm

8¾ (8¾, 9½, 9½)"
22 (22, 24, 24) cm

NOTES

- This sweater is worked in stranded two-color knitting (see page 26).

- The lower borders of the body and cuffs are worked in strips of garter stitch, then the cast-on and bound-off edges of the strips are joined to form rings. Stitches for the body are picked up along the selvedge of the lower border and worked in the round to the shoulders, with steeks for the armhole openings. The front neck shaping is sewn and cut during finishing. Stitches for the sleeves are picked up along the cuff selvedges and worked in the round, with facings at the upper edges to cover the raw edges of the steeked armhole openings.

BODY

Lower Border

With smaller dpn and C, CO 10 sts. Slipping the first st of every row knitwise with yarn in back, purling the last st, and knitting the center 8 sts for garter st (knit every row), work 16 (18, 20, 22) rows of each color in the following order: [C, D, E, F, G, H] 4 times, F, G—26 color blocks total completed; 8 (9, 10, 11) garter ridges in each block; piece measures about 33¼ (37½, 41½, 45¾)" (84.5 [95, 105.5, 116] cm) from CO. With RS facing, use another dpn to pick up 10 loops from CO end of border; these loops are just picked up and placed on the needle, not picked up and knitted. Hold dpns with live sts and picked-up sts tog with RS touching, being careful not to twist border, and use the three-needle bind-off method (see Glossary) to join the CO and BO ends so the border forms a ring. With A, longer cir needle in larger size, RS facing, and beg at border join, pick up and knit 208 (232, 260, 284) sts evenly along one selvedge of border (about 1 st for every garter ridge). Place marker (pm), and join for working in rnds; end-of-rnd m is at left side at start of front sts. With A, purl 1 rnd.

Next 2 rnds: *K2 with C, k2 with A; rep from * to end.

With A, knit 1 rnd, then purl 1 rnd, inc 44 (56, 64, 76) sts evenly spaced (about 1 st inc'd every 4 sts)—252 (288, 324, 360) sts; piece measures about 2" (5 cm) from lower selvedge of border. Work in patt from Stars chart, beg and end as shown and using accent colors for the X symbols on chart in first 36 rnds as foll: D for Rnds 1–9, C for Rnds 10–18, H for Rnds 19–27, and E for Rnds 28–36. After completing the first 36-rnd patt rep, use B for X symbols to end of body. Work even in chart patt until 90 (108, 108, 126) chart rnds have been completed, ending with Rnd 18 (36, 36, 18) of chart— piece measures about 13 (15, 15, 17¼)" (33 [38, 38, 44] cm) from lower selvedge of border.

0, 18) times, changing to shorter cir needle in larger size when there are too many sts to fit on dpn—135 (135, 167, 167) sts. Work even in patt from chart if necessary for your size until 126 (126, 126, 144) chart rnds have been completed, ending with Rnd 18 (18, 18, 36) of chart, or to about ¼" (6 mm) less than desired length. With B, knit 2 rnds—piece measures about 17½ (17½, 17½, 19½)" (44.5 [44.5, 44.5, 49.5] cm) from lower selvedge of cuff. With B, purl 1 rnd to mark start of armhole facing, then work in St st for ⅝" (1.5 cm) for facing. BO all sts.

FINISHING

Carefully steam-press pieces to measurements under a damp cloth. **Note:** Armhole facings are not shown on schematic.

Armhole Steeks

Baste a line of contrasting thread along the center of each 3-st steek. With sewing machine or by hand, sew a line of small straight stitches one stitch away on each side of the basting line. Sew over the same two lines of stitching again. Carefully cut open each armhole along the basting line.

Front Neck

Join 36 (43, 50, 56) shoulder sts of back and front using the three-needle bind-off method—54 (58, 62, 68) held sts rem at center back and front. Measure down 3¼" (8.5 cm) from exact center of front sts on holder. Baste the outline of a curved neck opening as shown by dotted line on schematic,

beg and ending the curve at the edges of the live front neck sts. Sew two lines of small straight stitches along the basting line. Cut out the neck shaping about ¼" (6 mm) inside the basting line to leave a small seam allowance.

Neckband

With A, shorter cir needle in smaller size, and RS facing, knit across 54 (58, 62, 68) held back neck sts dec 2 (2, 6, 8) sts evenly spaced, then pick up and knit 56 (60, 64, 68) sts along cut front neck edge, picking up below the sewing line so neckline stitching does not show on RS of garment—108 (116, 120, 128) sts. Pm and join for working in rnds. With A, purl 1 rnd.

Next 2 rnds: *K2 with B, k2 with A; rep from * to end.

With A, knit 1 rnd, then purl 1 rnd for neckband turning ridge. Work even in St st with A until piece measures ⅝" (1.5 cm) from turning ridge. Loosely BO all sts. Fold neckband facing to WS along turning ridge and sew invisibly in place so that it covers the cut front neck edge. Steam neckband carefully, if desired.

Sew sleeves into armholes, sewing between the first patt st and outermost steek st on the body, and sewing just below the purled ridge at the top of the sleeve so purled sleeve sts do not show on RS of garment. Sew facings at tops of sleeves invisibly on WS to conceal cut edges of steeks.

Weave in loose ends.

LA PAZ: PERUVIAN HATS AND BELTS

Lloyd Aero Bolivia took us over the Andes Mountains out from the desert around Articha in southern Peru. In the mystic twilight, we first glimpsed the contours of the Indians' geometric cultivation lands on the outskirts of La Paz, Bolivia's legendary capital. The thin air forced us to slow our pace, and we quickly learned that coca tea aided our breathing as we walked through the narrow and steep streets.

The city is a large marketplace. You can walk up and down streets between blue tarps, small tables filled with all kinds of wares for sale, and explosions of colors in the dresses, ponchos, and bowler hats of the Indians. Life in La Paz is lived on the street. Food is prepared side by side with the items to be sold. Each street has its own atmosphere and its own goods. One entire street is devoted to religious and magic goods where herbs, dye stuffs, and even dried llama fetuses are for sale. It is said that no handwork should be done in a house until an offering of a llama fetus has been laid in the foundation.

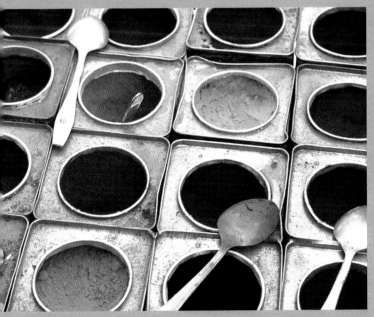

Dyes mimic the brilliant colors of plants and flowers.

LABYRINTH

Another motif that turns up on textiles and functional items all around the world is the meandering border or Greek scroll. Beloved children have many names, and I have chosen to call this motif "labyrinth." The child's sweater was inspired by a lovely cap that I found at a market in Peru.

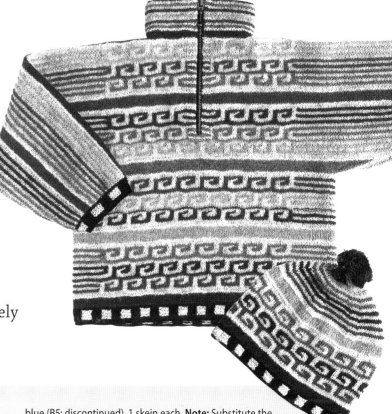

Finished Size
Sweater: About 25 (30½)" (63.5 [77.5] cm) chest circumference, to fit children's sizes 4 (8). Sweater shown photographed flat measures 30½" (77.5 cm).
Cap: About 13½ (15, 17½)" (34.5 [38, 44.5] cm) head circumference. Cap shown photographed flat measures 17½" (44.5 cm).

Yarn
About 100 (125) grams of a background color (A) and 50 grams each of five accent colors (B1, B2, B3, B4, and B5) of fingering-weight (#1 Super Fine) yarn.

Shown here
Isager Alpaca 2 (50% merino, 50% alpaca; 270 yd [247 m]/50 g): #2105 light gray heather (A), 2 (3) skeins; cerise (B1; discontinued), #014 orange (B2), aqua (B3; discontinued), #016 chartreuse (B4), and royal blue (B5; discontinued), 1 skein each. **Note:** Substitute the colors of your choice for the discontinued colors.

Needles
Size U.S. 2 (3 mm): 24" or 30" (60 or 75 cm) circular (cir). Adjust needle size if necessary to obtain the correct gauge.

Notions
Markers (m); stitch holder; tapestry needle; 6 (8)" (15 [20.5] cm) zipper; sharp-point sewing needle, contrasting basting thread, and matching sewing thread (for attaching zipper).

Gauge
29 stitches and 30 rows = 4" (10 cm) wide and 3" (7.5 cm) high in labyrinth pattern from charts; 26 stitches and about 50 rows = 4" (10 cm) in stockinette with garter stripes on each side of labyrinth patterns.

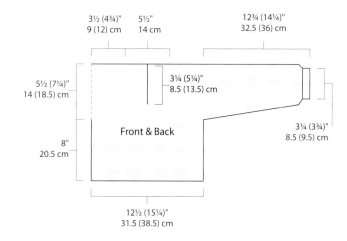

NOTES

- The sweater and cap borders are worked in stranded two-color garter stitch, the labyrinth patterns are worked in a combination of stockinette and slip stitch, and the body and sleeve stitches on each side of the labyrinth patterns are worked in stockinette with garter stripes.

- The sweater body is worked back and forth in rows in one piece beginning at the lower back, working up and over the shoulders with stitches cast on and bound off at each side for sleeves, and then down the front to the lower edge.

- When working labyrinth patterns, slip stitches as if to purl with yarn in back (pwise wyb) on right-side rows; slip stitches pwise with yarn in front (wyf) on wrong-side rows.

- For the labyrinth charts, use A for the background color throughout and change accent color B as indicated in the instructions.

- In the garter ridges on each side of the labyrinth pattern, whenever the two rows of a garter ridge are worked with different colors, the ridge will contain deliberate dashes of both colors on the RS. This gives a nice effect, but if you prefer solid-color garter ridges, you can knit both rows of the ridge using the same color; just remember to change to the correct color for working the center stitches of the labyrinth pattern.

- Always knit the first and last stitches of every row for selvedge stitches. If there is more than one color used in a row, knit the first and last stitches with both colors held together.

- The color sequences used here are just a suggestion—feel free to use your own colors and sequences.

- The scroll motifs in the sweaters shown on pages 72 and 79 are opposite those shown on the sweaters photographed flat on pages 73 and 80. The charts match the sweaters photographed flat.

- The scroll motifs in the cap shown on page 73 are opposite those on the cap on page 76. The Back chart used for the cap matches the one on page 76.

SWEATER

Lower Back

With B5, CO 90 (106) sts. Knit 3 rows, beg and ending with a WS row—2 garter ridges completed. Join A, and work stranded 2-color garter st for border as foll:

Row 1: (RS) K1 with A and B5 held tog (see Notes), k2 with B5, *k4 with A, k4 with B5; rep from * to last 7 sts, k4 with A, k2 with B5, k1 with A and B5 held tog.

Row 2: (WS) K1 with A and B5 held tog, k2 with B5, bring B5 to front, *k4 with A, bring A to front, k4 with B5, bring B5 to front; rep from * to last 7 sts, k4 with A, k2 with B5, k1 with A and B5 held tog.

Rep the last 2 rows 2 more times—3 two-color garter ridges completed. With B5, knit 2 rows, inc 0 (4) sts evenly spaced in second row—90 (110) sts; 6 garter ridges total; piece measures about 1" (2.5 cm) from CO. With B1, work in St st for 6 rows, knitting first and last st of each row (see Notes), and placing markers (pm) on each side of center 70 (80) sts in last row—10 (15) sts on each side of marked center sts. **Note:** When working in patt from Labyrinth charts, work the sts on each side of the marked center sts as shown by "side sts" on charts. The charts have only 2 side sts at each end to indicate the patt for all the side sts; work as many body or sleeve sts as you have in the patt shown, keeping selvedge sts in garter st throughout. Work 38 rows in patt from Labyrinth Back chart, using B2 as accent color for Rows 5–13, B1 for Rows 14–22, and B3 for Rows 25–34. With B4, work 6 rows St st. Work 38 rows in patt from Labyrinth Back chart, using B1 for Rows 5–13, B4 for Rows 14–22, and B2 for Rows 25–34—piece measures about 8" (20.5 cm) from CO for both sizes. Mark each end of last row with waste yarn to indicate beg of armholes.

Sleeves

With B3, work 6 rows in St st and *at the same time* use the backward-loop method (see Glossary) to CO 10 (9) sts at end first 2 rows and to CO 6 (7) sts at the end of next 4 rows—134 (156) sts total; 22 (23) sleeve sts at each side. **Note:** CO for sleeve cont into next chart patt; read the next section all the way through before proceeding. Work 38 rows in patt from Labyrinth Back chart, using B4 for Rows 5–13, B3 for Rows 14–22, and B1 for Rows 25–34. *At the same time* CO 6 (7) sts at end of first 18 rows of chart with color in use, working new sts in patt for side sts—242 (282) sts; 76 (86) sleeve sts; 90 (110) back sts. With B2, work 6 rows in St st. Cont as foll for your size:

Try out color combinations on a gauge swatch.

Size 25" Only

Work 19 rows in patt from Labyrinth Back chart, using B3 for Rows 5–13 and B2 for Rows 14–19, ending with a RS row—piece measures about 5½" (14 cm) from beg of armholes and 13½" (34.5 cm) from CO. Place center 40 sts on holder for back neck—101 sts rem at each side. Working each side separately, work Rows 20 and 21 of Labyrinth Front chart using B2 for accent color in Row 21 and using the backward-loop method to CO 20 sts at each neck edge—242 sts; 121 sts on each side of neck slit.

The cap incorporates all of the stitch patterns used in the sweater.

Next row: (WS) Beg and ending where indicated and cont with B2 for accent color, work Row 22 of Labyrinth Front chart to last 4 sts at left neck edge, k4; work first 4 sts at right neck edge as k4, work in patt to end. Keeping 4 sts at each neck edge in garter st, work Rows 23–38 of Labyrinth Front chart, using B2 for Rows 23–25 and B3 for Rows 26–34.

With B2, work 6 rows in St st with garter neck edge sts. Work 20 rows in patt from Labyrinth Front chart, using B1 for Rows 5–14 and B3 for Rows 17–20—piece measures about 3¼" (8.5 cm) from where back neck sts were put on hold. **Note:** From here on, work across all sts with a single strand of yarn to close bottom of neck slit. Working center 8

sts in garter st for border at base of neck slit and BO 6 sts at beg of each row, work Rows 21–26 of chart, using B3 for Rows 21–25, and B4 for Row 26—206 sts rem. Resume working center 8 sts in established chart patt. Work Rows 27–38 of chart, using B4 for Rows 27–34 and BO 6 sts at beg of every row—134 sts rem. With B3, work 6 rows in St st and *at the same time* BO 6 sts at beg of first 4 rows, then BO 10 sts at beg of next 2 rows—90 sts rem; armhole measures about 5½" (14 cm) from where back neck sts were put on holder. Mark each end of last row with waste yarn to indicate base of armholes.

Size 30½" Only

Work 38 rows in patt from Labyrinth Back chart, using B3 for Rows 5–13, B2 for Rows 14–22, and B4 for Rows 25–34. With B1, work 3 rows in St st, ending with a RS row—piece measures about 7¼" (18.5 cm) from beg of armholes and 15¼" (38.5 cm) from CO. Place center 40 sts on holder for back neck—121 sts rem at each side. Working each side separately, work 2 rows in St st with B1, using the backward-loop method to CO 20 sts at each neck edge—282 sts; 141 sts on each side of neck slit.

Next row: (WS) With B1, work in patt to last 4 sts at left neck edge, k4; work first 4 sts at right neck edge as k4, work in patt to end. Keeping 4 sts at each neck edge in garter st, work 38 rows in patt from Labyrinth Front chart, beg and ending where indicated, and using B4 for Rows 5–14, B2 for Rows 17–25, and B3 for Rows 26–34.

With B2, work 6 rows in St st with garter neck edge sts. Work 20 rows in patt from Labyrinth Front chart, using B1 for Rows 5–14 and B3 for Rows 17–20—piece measures about 5¼" (13.5 cm) from where back neck sts were put on hold. **Note:** From here on, work across all sts with a single strand of yarn to close bottom of neck slit. Working center 8 sts in garter st for border at base of neck slit·and BO 7 sts at beg of each row, work Rows 21–26 of chart, using B3 for Rows 21–25, and B4 for Row 26 — 240 sts. Resume working center 8 sts in established chart patt. Work Rows 27–38 of chart, using B4 for Rows 27–34 and BO 7 sts at beg of every row—156 sts rem. With B3, work 6 rows in St st and *at the same time* BO 7 sts at beg of first 4 rows, then BO 9 sts at beg of next 2 rows—110 sts rem; armhole measures about 7¼" (18.5 cm) from where back neck sts were put on holder. Mark each end of last row with waste yarn to indicate base of armholes.

Lower Front

For both sizes, work 38 rows in patt from Labyrinth Front chart, using B2 for Rows 5–14, B4 for Rows 17–25, and B1 for Rows 26–34. With B4, work 6 rows in St st. Work 38 rows in patt from Labyrinth Front chart, using B3 for Rows 5–14, B1 for Rows 17–25, and B2 for Rows 26–34. With B1, work 6 rows in St st, ending with a WS row—piece measures about 7" (18 cm) from base of armholes. With B5, knit 2 rows, dec 0 (4) sts evenly spaced in first row—90 (106) sts. With B5 and A, rep Rows 1 and 2 of lower back border 3 times. With B5,

The pattern for Labyrinth was inspired by a cap found in a Peruvian market.

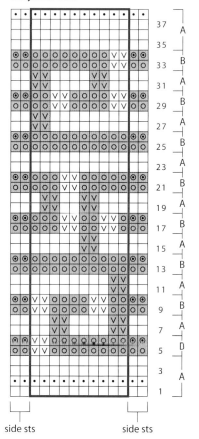

Labyrinth Back

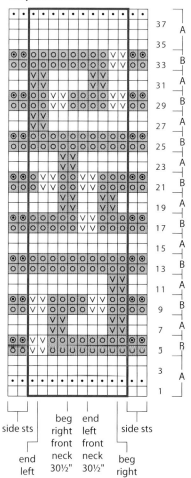

Labyrinth Front

A: k on RS; p on WS

• A: k on WS

v A: sl 1 wyb on RS; sl 1 wyf on WS

○ B: k on RS; p on WS

⊙ B: k on WS

v B: sl 1 wyb on RS; sl 1 wyf on WS

☐ pattern repeat

knit 3 rows, beg and ending with a RS row—piece measures about 8" (20.5 cm) from end of armholes. With B5, BO all sts kwise with WS facing.

Cuffs

With B5 and RS facing, pick up and knit 42 (50) sts evenly spaced along cuff selvedge. With B5, knit 1 WS row. With B5 and A, rep Rows 1 and 2 of lower back border 3 times. With B5, knit 3 rows, beg and ending with a RS row—cuff measures about 1" (2.5 cm) from pick-up row; sleeve measures 12¾ (14¼)" (32.5 [36] cm) from edge of body. With B5, BO all sts kwise with WS facing. Rep for other cuff.

FINISHING

Block to measurements; right sleeve is not shown on schematic. With A threaded on a tapestry needle, use the mattress st (see Glossary) to sew sleeve and side seams. Carefully steam-press seams.

Back

Neckband and Facing

With B1, RS facing, and beg at right edge of neck opening, pick up and knit 20 sts along sts CO at right front neck, k40 held back neck sts, then pick up and knit 20 sts along CO at left front neck—80 sts total.

With B1, knit 1 WS row. Work garter and St st stripes for 26 rows as foll: 2 rows St st with B1, 2 rows garter st with A, 2 rows garter st with B3, 2 rows St st with A, 2 rows garter st with B2, 2 rows St st with A, 2 rows garter st with B4, 2 rows St st with A, 2 rows garter st with B1, 2 rows St st with A, 2 rows garter st with B3, 2 rows St st with A, and 2 rows garter st with B5—neckband measures about 2¼" (5.5 cm) from pick-up row; last row of B5 is turning ridge for neckband facing. Cont in St st with B5 until facing measures 2¼" (5.5 cm) from turning ridge, ending with a WS row.

Next row: (RS) With B5, k20, join second strand of yarn, BO center 40 sts, knit to end—20 sts rem each side.

Working each side separately, cont in St st with B5 and *at the same time* dec 1 st on each side of center gap every 4th row 10 times—10 sts at each side. Work even in St st until facing measures 6½ (8½)" (16.5 [21.5] cm) from turning ridge, or about ½" (1.3 cm) longer than zipper. BO all sts. Fold facing to WS along turning ridge and, with B5 threaded on a tapestry needle, sew 40 BO sts in center of facing to pick-up row of back neck on WS. Leave facing extensions free for now. Weave in loose ends.

Zipper

Pin zipper to front opening so zipper teeth show between garter edges of neck slit and top of zipper is aligned with turning ridge of neckband; bottom of zipper may extend below base of neck slit. Baste zipper in place as described on page 157. With sewing needle and matching thread, sew in zipper with small backstitches placed close to selvedges of garter neck edging on the right side. With sewing needle and thread, sew selvedges of facing extensions to zipper tape on WS, taking care that facing does not catch in zipper.

CAP

With B5, CO 98 (106, 130) sts. Knit 1 WS row. With B5 and A, rep Rows 1 and 2 of lower back border 3 times. With B5, knit 2 rows, ending with a WS row and inc 4 (6, 2) sts evenly spaced in second row—102 (112, 132) sts; 5 garter ridges total; piece measures about ¾" (2 cm) from CO. With B1, work in St st for 6 rows, knitting first and last st of each row (see Notes). Work 38 rows in patt from Labyrinth Back chart, using B2 as accent color for Rows 5–13, B1 for Rows 14–22, and B3 for Rows 25–34. Work 6 rows in St st with B4, then work 2 rows garter st with A. Work 2 rows in St st with A, dec 0 (0, 4) sts evenly spaced—102 (112, 128) sts. Work 2 rows garter st with B2—piece measures about 5¼" (13.5 cm) from CO.

Crown

Row 1: (RS) With A, *k2, ssk, k14 (16, 15), k2tog, place marker (pm); rep from * to last 2 sts, k2—92 (102, 116) sts; 18 (20, 19) sts each in 5 (5, 6) marked sections and 2 sts at end.

Row 2: With A, purl.

Rows 3 and 4: With B2, knit.

Row 5: With A, *k2, ssk, knit to 2 sts before m, k2tog, slip marker (sl m); rep from * to last 2 sts, k2—10 (10, 12) sts dec'd.

Row 6: With A, purl.

Rows 7–30 (34, 30): Rep Rows 3–6 six (seven, six) more times, working garter ridge in Rows 3 and 4 using B1 twice, then B3 twice, then B4 two (three, two) times—22 (22, 32) sts rem; 4 (4, 5) sts each in 5 (5, 6) marked sections and 2 sts at end. Cont for your size as foll:

Sizes 13½ (15)" Only

Knit 2 rows with B4 (B1).

Next row: (RS) With A, *k1, k3tog; rep from * to last 2 sts, k2—12 sts rem for both sizes.

Purl 1 WS row with A, then knit 2 rows with B1.

Next row: (RS) With A, *k2tog; rep from * to end—6 sts.

Size 17½" Only

Knit 2 rows with B1.

Next row: (RS) With A, *k2, k3tog; rep from * to last 2 sts, k2—20 sts rem.

Purl 1 WS row with A, then knit 2 rows with B1.

Next row: (RS) With A, *k2tog; rep from * to end—10 sts.

FINISHING

Cut yarn, thread A on a tapestry needle, draw through rem sts, pull tight, and fasten off on WS. Weave in loose ends. With A threaded on a tapestry needle and using the mattress st (see Glossary), sew center back seam. Using all 5 accent colors, make a 2½" (6.5 cm) pom-pom (see Glossary) and attach it to the top of the cap as shown.

CATS

The idea for using positive and negative fields on this sweater came from a woven belt. The belt has a bird motif, but I substituted a cat motif that appears frequently in Incan textiles.

Finished Size
About 37½ (45, 52½)" (95 [114.5, 133.5] cm) chest circumference. Sweater shown photographed flat measures 52½" (133.5 cm).

Yarn
About 150 (175, 200) grams each of two light main colors (A1 and A2), 150 (175, 200) grams each of two dark main colors (B1 and B2), and 30 (40, 50) grams each of two accent colors (C and D) of fingering-weight (#1 Super Fine) yarn.

Shown here
Isager Wool 1 (100% wool; 340 yd [310 m]/50 g): #3s light tan heather (A1) and #2s light gray heather, 3 (4, 4) skeins each; #47 steel gray (B1) and #4s charcoal (B2), 3 (4, 4) skeins each.

Isager Alpaca 2 (50% merino, 50% alpaca; 270 yd [247 m]/50 g): #012 grayed olive (C) and #016 chartreuse (D), 1 skein each.

Needles
Body and sleeves—size U.S. 6 (4 mm): 16" and 24" (40 and 60 cm) circular (cir) and set of 4 or 5 double-pointed (dpn). *Facings*—size U.S. 4 (3.5 mm): 16" and 24" (40 and 60 cm) cir and set of 4 or 5 dpn. *Welts*—size U.S. 2 (3 mm): two 24" (60 cm) cir. Adjust needle size if necessary to obtain the correct gauge.

Notions
Markers (m); stitch holders; cable needle (cn); tapestry needle; sharp-point sewing needle or sewing machine; contrasting basting thread; matching sewing thread.

Gauge
56 stitches (one pattern repeat wide) and 40 rounds (5 pattern repeats high) measure about 7½" (19 cm) wide and 6¼" (16 cm) high in pattern from Stripes and Cable chart on largest needles, worked in rounds; 29½ stitches and 26 rounds = 4" (10 cm) in vertical stripe pattern of sleeves on largest needles, worked in rounds; 6 stitches in cable pattern of sleeves measure about ½" (1.3 cm) wide on largest needles, worked in rounds.

STITCH GUIDE

Cable

(worked over 6 sts)

Rnds 1–3: K3 with B, k3 with A.

Rnd 4: Sl 3 B sts to cable needle (cn) and hold in front, k3 with A, k3 with B from cn.

Rnds 5–7: K3 with A, k3 with B.

Rnd 8: Sl 3 A sts to cn and hold in front, k3 with B, k3 with A from cn.

Rep Rnds 1–8 for patt.

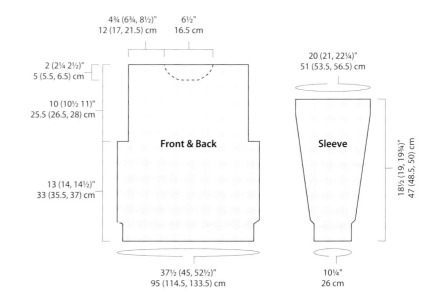

4¾ (6¾, 8½)"
12 (17, 21.5) cm

6½"
16.5 cm

2 (2¼ 2½)"
5 (5.5, 6.5) cm

10 (10½ 11)"
25.5 (26.5, 28) cm

Front & Back

13 (14, 14½)"
33 (35.5, 37) cm

37½ (45, 52½)"
95 (114.5, 133.5) cm

20 (21, 22¼)"
51 (53.5, 56.5) cm

Sleeve

18½ (19, 19¾)"
47 (48.5, 50) cm

10¼"
26 cm

NOTES

- This sweater is worked in stranded two-color knitting (see page 26).

- The body is worked in the round to the shoulder line, with steeks for the armhole openings. The front neck shaping is stitched and cut during finishing. The sleeves are worked in the round, with facings at the upper edges to cover the raw edges of the steeked armhole openings.

- The main colors A and B are both made up of two different-colored strands held together. Use one strand each of A1 and A2 held together for color A and one strand each of B1 and B2 held together for color B. Colors C and D are used as single strands.

- The manner in which you handle the yarns for the vertical stripe sections causes the stitches of one color to be slightly larger than the stitches of the other, so they "pop" out from the background on the right side of the fabric. The slightly more prominent stitches are said to be in the dominant color.

- For this project, colors A and B alternate as the dominant color in the striped sections. Experiment with a gauge swatch until you can achieve the desired effect and notice how you hold and manipulate the yarns to determine what causes one color to be dominant. Use the colors in the same manner when working in the round or on right-side rows. When purling wrong-side rows (as for the top of the sleeve), reverse the positions of the two colors in order to keep the correct color dominant on the right side.

- For the Front and Back Cats charts, the color used for each cat motif should be worked in the dominant color, so the colors exchange positions between the individual cat panels.

BODY

With C and longer cir needle in middle size, CO 200
(220, 230) sts. Place marker (pm) and join for working in rnds, being careful not to twist sts. Work even
in St st (knit every round) until piece measures 2¼"
(5.5 cm) from CO. Change to A. Knit 1 rnd, then purl
1 rnd for turning ridge. Change to longer cir needle
in largest size and work in St st for 2¼" (5.5 cm) from
turning ridge.

Inc rnd: Knit, inc 80 (116, 162) sts evenly spaced
(about 4 [6, 10] sts inc'd for every 10 [11, 14]
sts)—280 (336, 392) sts.

Join B and work in patt from Stripe and Cable chart
until piece measures 13 (14, 14½)" (33 [35.5, 37] cm)
from turning ridge, or desired length to armhole.

Armhole Steeks

K1 in patt, BO next 20 stripe sts for left armhole,
work in patt until there are 120 (148, 176) sts on
right-hand needle after BO gap, BO next 20 stripe sts
for right armhole, work in patt to first st of rnd (the
st before BO gap) and knit this st in patt again— 240
(296, 352) sts total; 120 (148, 176) sts each for front
and back; 7 sts on each side of both armhole gaps
should be 1 stripe st at the edge with a 6-st cable
just inside it.

Next rnd: *Pm, use the backward-loop method (see
Glossary) to CO 4 steek sts alternating 1 st of each
color, pm,* work in established patt to next BO gap;
rep from * to * for second steek, work in patt to
end—248 (304, 360) sts total; 120 (148, 176) sts

Positive and negative motifs are common in Peru, as shown
in this woven belt.

each for front and back; 4 steek sts at base of each
armhole; rnd beg at start of left armhole steek.

On the foll rnds, work the 4 steek sts at each side in a
solid color, 1×1 checkerboard patt, or stripes, as you
prefer in order to distinguish them from the patt sts.
Cont in established patt until armholes measure 5
(5¼, 5½)" (12.5 [13.5, 14] cm).

Welt

Welts are worked using the intarsia method (see page 53) with a separate bobbin or butterfly of yarn for each color block; twist the yarns at each color change to prevent leaving holes. Wind 4 (4, 6) butterflies with C and 4 (6, 6) butterflies with D. Change to smallest cir needle.

Sizes 37½ (52½)" Only

Work 4 steek sts then k32 with D, [k28 with C, k28 with D] 1 (2) time(s), k32 with C, join a new butterfly of C, work 4 steek sts then k32 with C, [k28 with D, k28 with C] 1 (2) time(s), k32 with D.

Size 45" Only

*Work 4 steek sts then k32 with D, k28 with C, k28 with D, k28 with C, k32 with D; rep from * once more.

All Sizes

Working sts in their matching colors, knit 5 rnds. With WS facing, slip the second smallest cir needle into each purl bump along the first intarsia rnd; these loops are just picked up and placed on the needle, not picked up and knitted—248 (304, 360) picked-up loops on second cir needle. Hold needles tog and parallel with RS facing, live sts on front needle, and picked-up loops on back needle. Using matching colors, *insert right-hand tip of needle into first st on both needles and k2tog (1 st from each needle); rep from * to end—248 (304, 360) sts on working needle; all picked-up loops have been joined.

Cats Pattern

Wind 4 (4, 6) butterflies with A and 4 (6, 6) butterflies with B. Change to longer cir needle in largest size. Work Rnd 1 of Front and Back Cats charts for your size using the intarsia method as foll:

Sizes 37½ (52½)" Only

Work 4 steek sts with B, then for Front Cats chart k32 with B, [k28 with A, k28 with B] 1 (2) time(s), k32 with A, join a new butterfly of A, work 4 steek sts with A, then for Back Cats chart k32 with A, [k28 with B, k28 with A] 1 (2) time(s), k32 with B.

Size 45" Only

Work 4 steek sts with B, then for Front and Back Cats chart k32 with B, k28 with A, k28 with B, k28 with A, k32 with B; rep from * once more.

All Sizes

Knit all sts in their matching colors for Rnd 2 of chart. Cut off all except one butterfly each of A and B and work Rnds 3–14 of chart in stranded two-color knitting. Rejoin rem butterflies as needed and work Rnds 15 and 16 of chart in intarsia as for Rnds 1 and 2. Change to smallest cir needle, rejoin butterflies of C and D, and work another welt the same as the welt below the Cats charts—248 (304, 360) sts on working needle; all picked-up loops have been joined; armholes measure about 7½ (7¾, 8)" (19 [19.5, 20.5] cm). Change to longer cir needle in largest size and one ball each of A and B. Resume working Stripes and Cable patt with steek sts as for the sts below the first welt, but do not

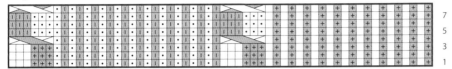

Stripes and Cable

•	A dominant
☐	A not dominant
+	B dominant
I	B not dominant
■	pattern repeat

sl 3 B sts to cn and hold in front, k3 with A, k3 with B from cn

sl 3 A sts to cn and hold in front, k3 with B, k3 with A from cn

Front Cats Sizes 37½" and 52½"

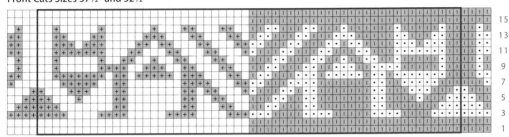

Back Cats Sizes 37½" and 52½"

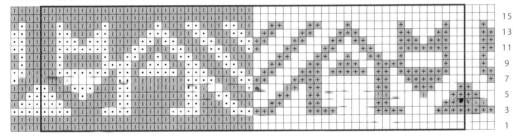

Front and Back Cats Size 45"

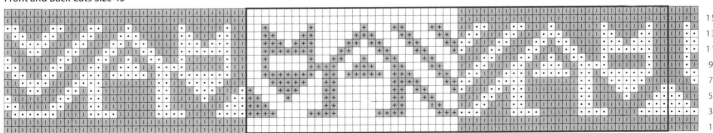

work the center 1 (2, 1) cable(s) on the front because the front neckline will cut into these sts; work the sts of the omitted front cable(s) in established stripes instead. Work the back sts entirely in patt, including all cables. Cont in patt for 2½ (2¾, 3)" (6.5 [7, 7.5] cm) from welt above Cats charts—armholes measure about 10 (10½, 11)" (25.5 [26.5, 28] cm). Change to smallest cir needle, rejoin butterflies of C and D, and work another welt the same as the first two welts—248 (304, 360) sts on working

needle; all picked-up loops have been joined. Cut off yarns. Place steek sts on holders. Place 36 (50, 64) shoulder sts at armhole edges of front and back on holders, then place rem 48 center front and back sts on separate holders.

LEFT SLEEVE

With D and dpn in middle size, CO 50 sts for all sizes. Pm, and join for working in rnds, being careful not to twist sts. Work even in St st until piece measures 2¼" (5.5 cm) from CO. Change to A. Knit 1 rnd, then purl 1 rnd for turning ridge. Change to dpn in largest size, and work in St st for 2¼" (5.5 cm) from turning ridge.

Inc rnd: Knit, inc 30 sts evenly spaced (about 2 inc'd sts for every 3 sts)—80 sts.

Next rnd: Join B, work Cable patt (see Stitch guide) over 6 sts, pm, with B as the dominant color [k1 with B, k1 with A] 17 times, pm, work Cable patt over 6 sts, pm, with A as the dominant color [k1 with B, k1 with A] 17 times.

Cont in established patts and *at the same time* inc 1 st on each side of cable at beg of rnd every 3 rnds 19 (15, 12) times, then every 2 rnds 17 (25, 32) times, working new sts into stripe patts and changing to progressively longer cir needle in largest size when there are too many sts to fit on dpn—152 (160, 168) sts; piece measures about 16½ (17, 17¾)" (42 [43, 45] cm) from turning ridge. Change to working back and forth in rows. Work even in patt in rows until piece measures 18½ (19, 19¾)"

Back

(47 [48.5, 50] cm) from turning ridge, ending with a RS row. Knit 1 WS row with B to mark start of armhole facing, then cont in St st with B for ⅝" (1.5 cm) for facing. BO all sts.

RIGHT SLEEVE

Work facing, cuff, and inc rnd as for left sleeve—80 sts.

Next rnd: Join B, work Cable patt over 6 sts, pm, with A as the dominant color [k1 with B, k1 with A] 17 times, pm, work Cable patt over 6 sts, pm, with B as the dominant color [k1 with B, k1 with A] 17 times—stripe sections will have dominant colors arranged opposite from how they appear in left sleeve.

Complete as for left sleeve.

FINISHING

Carefully steam-press pieces to measurements under a damp cloth. **Note:** Sleeve is shown in the round on the schematic even though the final 2" (5 cm) is worked in rows below the facing turning ridge; lower body, cuff, and armhole facings are not shown on schematic.

Steeks

Baste a line of contrasting thread along the center of each 4-st steek. With sewing machine or by hand, sew a line of small straight stitches one stitch away on both sides of the basting line. Sew over the same two lines of stitching again. Carefully cut open each armhole along the basting line.

Front Neck

Join 36 (50, 64) shoulder sts of back and front with their matching colors using the three-needle bind-off method (see Glossary)—48 held sts rem at center back and front. Measure down 2 (2¼, 2½)" (5 [5.5, 6.5] cm) from exact center of front sts on holder, about ½" (1.3 cm) above second welt. Baste the outline of a curved neck opening as shown by dotted line on schematic, beg and ending the curve at the edges of the live front neck sts. Sew two lines of small straight stitches along the basting line. Cut out the neck shaping about ⅝" (1.5 cm) inside the basting line to leave a small seam allowance.

Neckband

Neckband is worked in St st intarsia. Wind 2 butterflies each of A, B, C, and D. With shorter cir needle in largest size, knit across first 24 held back sts with A, knit across rem 24 held back sts with B, then pick up and knit 64 sts along cut front neck edge using A for first 32 sts and B for next 32 sts, and picking up below the sewing line so neckline stitching does not show on RS of garment—112 sts. Pm and join for working in rnds. Working sts in their matching colors, work in St st until piece measures 1½" (3.8 cm) from pick-up rnd. With matching colors, purl 1 rnd for turn-ing ridge, then knit 1 rnd. Cut off yarns. Change to shorter cir needle in middle size.

Next rnd: K24 with D, k24 with C, k32 with D, k32 with C.

Rep the last rnd until piece measures 1½" (3.8 cm) from turning ridge. BO all sts loosely. Fold neckband facing to WS along turning ridge and sew invisibly in place so that it covers the cut front neck edge.

Arrange body and sleeves so the lighter A-dominant stripe sections of each sleeve correspond to the front of the body and the darker B-dominant sections cor-respond to the back. Sew sleeves into armholes, sew-ing between the first patt st and outermost steek st on the body and sewing just below the purled ridge at the top of the sleeve so purled sleeve sts do not show on RS of garment. **Note:** Smooth the welts above and below Cats charts downward, but allow welts at shoulders to stand up on either side of shoulder join so join lies in the "valley" between the back and front welts as shown in photograph. Sew facings at tops of sleeves invisibly on WS to conceal cut edges of steeks. Sew short selvedges at tops of sleeves to BO sts at base of armholes. Fold lower body and cuff facings to WS along turning ridges and sew invisibly in place.

Weave in loose ends. Steam-press seams, facings, and welts carefully.

LAKE TITICACA: PONCHOS

Sucre, located in the region near Copacabana in Lake Titicaca, is the home of colorful striped ponchos. Inspired by these ponchos, I decided to combine stripes with zigzag patterns. These zigzag patterns are worked by increasing and decreasing stitches within individual stripes. If there is the same number of increases as decreases, the stitch count (and the width) remains constant. If, however, you omit some decreases, the piece will become wider; if you omit some increases, the piece will become narrower. In this way, it's possible to shape the garment. It's also easy to adjust the length of the body and sleeves if the piece is worked from the top down.

On the island of Taquile in Lake Titicaca, the people live primarily from the land—they knit and weave for extra income. On this island, the men knit and the women weave. I have been very fortunate to have visited the island in connection with a knitting workshop and have incorporated a traditional pattern from the island in one of my garment designs.

The striped poncho is the foundation of Peruvian outerwear.

SUCRE

The colorful stripes around
the lower edge of this simple
cardigan were inspired by the
ponchos of Lake Titicaca.

Finished Size
About 41½ (46)" (105.5 [117] cm) bust circumference, with a
1¾ (1½)" (4.5 [3.8] cm) gap at center front. **Note:** Adjust amount
of gap to accommodate smaller or larger sizes.

Yarn
About 250 (300) grams each of two dark main colors
(A1 and A2), and 40 (50) grams each of three bright colors
(B, C, and D) of fingering-weight (#1 Super Fine) yarn.

Shown here
Isager Alpaca 2 (50% merino, 50% alpaca; 270 yd [247 m]/50 g):
#500 black (A1), 5 (6) skeins; tomato (B; discontinued), turquoise
(C; discontinued), and cerise (D; discontinued), 1 skein each. **Note:** Sub-
stitute the colors of your choice for the discontinued colors.

Isager Wool 1 (100% wool; 340 yd [310 m]/50 g): #55 plum
(A2), 5 (6) skeins.

Needles
Size U.S. 6 (4 mm): straight and set of 2 double-pointed (dpn).
Adjust needle size if necessary to obtain the correct gauge.

Notions
Markers (m); stitch holders; tapestry needle; decorative pin for
closure (optional).

Gauge
20 stitches and 38 rows = 4" (10 cm) in garter stitch; 18 (22, 26, 34,
38)-st chevrons measure about 3¼ (4, 4¾, 6¼ 7)" (8.5 [10, 12, 16,
18] cm) wide; 15 (19)-st front edge triangles measure about 2¼
(2¾)" (5.5 [7] cm) wide; 34 rows = 4" (10 cm) for chevrons and front
edge triangles. Gauges given are with two strands of yarn held
together; see Notes on page 95 for measuring chevrons.

STITCH GUIDE

Chevron Base Triangle
CO 4 sts.

Row 1: (WS) Knit into front and back of first st (k1f&b), place marker (pm), sl 2 sts purlwise with yarn in front (pwise wyf), pm, k1f&b—6 sts.

Row 2: (RS) Knit to 1 st before m, k1f&b, slip marker (sl m), k2, sl m, k1f&b, knit to end—2 sts inc'd.

Row 3: K1f&b, knit to m, sl m, sl 2 pwise wyf, sl m, knit to last st, k1f&b—2 sts inc'd.

Rep Rows 2 and 3 as required to equal the total number of rows given in the directions, ending with WS Row 3—4 sts inc'd each time Rows 2 and 3 are repeated; final st count will be a multiple of 4 sts + 2.

Left Front Edge Triangle
CO 3 sts.

Row 1: (WS) Sl 1 pwise wyf, [k1f&b] 2 times—5 sts.

Row 2: (RS) Knit.

Row 3: Sl 1 pwise wyf, k1f&b, knit to last st, k1f&b—2 sts inc'd.

Rep Rows 2 and 3 as required to equal the total number of rows given in the directions, ending with WS Row 3—2 sts inc'd each time Rows 2 and 3 are repeated; final st count will be an odd number of sts.

Right Front Edge Triangle
CO 3 sts.

Row 1: (WS) [K1f&b] 2 times, k1—5 sts.

Row 2: (RS) Sl 1 pwise with yarn in back (wyb), k1f&b, knit to last st, k1f&b—2 sts inc'd.

Row 3: Knit.

Rep Rows 2 and 3 as required to equal the total number of rows given in the directions, ending with WS Row 3—2 sts inc'd each time Rows 2 and 3 are repeated; final st count will be an odd number of sts.

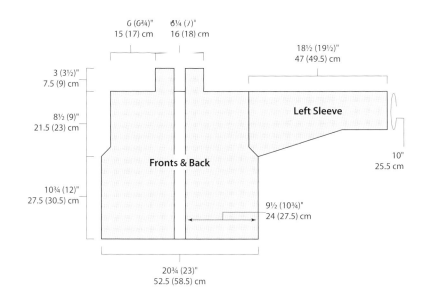

NOTES

- All four colors are made up of two strands of yarn held together throughout. Use one strand each of A1 and A2 held together for color A; use a double strand of the same yarn for colors B, C, and D.

- Each chevron section is worked on the bias with increases each side of one slip-stitch column and decreases each side of the next slip-stitch column to create the zigzag effect shown.

- When working in the chevron pattern, the fabric will be forced into a straight line while it is still on the needles; after you have worked a few inches, it will start to assume its final zigzag appearance. To measure the width of a chevron segment, do not measure along the bias lines of the tilted garter ridges. Instead, lay a ruler straight across connecting the center of the 2-stitch slip-stitch columns at each end of the upside down V in a complete chevron, then measure the distance between the centers of the slip-stitch columns.

- To measure the height of a chevron section, measure straight up along a single slip-stitch column. When checking gauge, remember that each slip stitch visible on the right side counts as two rows.

Stripes turn into zigzags when worked in combination with increases and decreases.

LEFT FRONT

With A, CO 4 sts and work Chevron Base Triangle patt (see Stitch Guide) for 7 rows for both sizes— 18 sts. Break yarn and place sts on holder. With A, CO 4 sts and work Chevron Base Triangle patt for 9 (11) rows—22 (26) sts. Break yarn and place sts on holder. With A, CO 3 sts and work Left Edge Triangle patt (see Stitch Guide) for 11 (15) rows—15 (19) sts. Break yarn and place sts on holder. Place all 3 triangles on needle with RS facing so that on the next RS row the 18-st triangle will be worked first, followed

11 (15) rows—15 (19) sts. Break yarn and place sts on holder. Place all three triangles on needle with RS facing so that on the next RS row the 15 (19)-st edge triangle will be worked first, followed by the 22 (26)-st triangle, then the 18-st triangle—55 (63) sts total. Join A with RS facing.

Joining row: (RS) Sl 1 pwise wyb, k1f&b, k10 (14), k2tog, pm, k1 (last st of edge triangle), k1 (first st of next triangle), pm, k2tog, k6 (8), k1f&b, sl m, k2, sl m, k1f&b, k6 (8), k2tog, pm, k1 (last st of triangle), k1 (first st of next triangle), pm, k2tog, k4, k1f&b, sl m, k2, sl m, k1f&b, k4, k2tog, k1 (side edge st)—still 55 (63) sts.

Next row: (WS) *Knit to marked sts, sl m, sl 2 pwise wyf, sl m; rep from * 3 more times, knit to end.

Cont in patt as foll:

Row 1: (RS) With A, sl 1 pwise wyb, k1f&b, k10 (14), k2tog, sl m, k2, sl m, k2tog, k6 (8), k1f&b, sl m, k2, sl m, k1f&b, k6 (8), k2tog, sl m, k2, sl m, k2tog, k4, k1f&b, sl m, k2, sl m, k1f&b, k4, k2tog, k1.

Row 2: (WS) With A, *knit to marked sts, sl m, sl 2 pwise wyf, sl m; rep from * 3 more times, knit to end.

Rows 3–8: Rep Rows 1 and 2 three more times.

Rows 9–14: With B, rep Rows 1 and 2 three times.

Ponchos offer an endless array of stripe patterns.

Row 15: With A, rep Row 1.

Row 16: With A, sl 1 pwise wyf, *purl to marked sts, sl m, sl 2 pwise wyf, sl m; rep from * 3 more times, purl to end last st, k1.

Rows 17–22: With B, rep Rows 1 and 2 three times.

Rows 23–28: With C, rep Rows 1 and 2 three times.

Rows 29 and 30: With A, rep Rows 15 and 16.

Rows 31–36: With C, rep Rows 1 and 2 three times.

Rows 37–42: With D, rep Rows 1 and 2 three times.

Rows 43 and 44: With A, rep Rows 15 and 16.

Rows 45–50: With D, rep Rows 1 and 2 three times.

Rows 51–90 (100): With A, rep Rows 1 and 2—92 (102) total rows from joining row (including joining row); piece measures about 10¾ (12)" (27.5 [30.5] cm) from joining row.

Shape Armhole

(RS) Sl 1 pwise wyb, k1f&b, k10 (14), k2tog, sl m, k2, sl m, k2tog, k6 (8), k1f&b, sl m, k2, sl m, k1f&b, k6 (8), k2tog, sl m, k2, sl m, k2tog, k4, k1f&b, sl m, k2, sl m, k1, place last 7 sts on holder for right front armhole—48 (56) sts rem.

Next row: (WS) K1 (armhole edge st), *sl m, sl 2 pwise wyf, sl m, knit to marked sts; rep from * 2 more times, sl m, sl 2 pwise wyf, sl m, knit to end.

Next row: (RS) Sl 1 pwise wyb, k1f&b, k10 (14), k2tog, sl m, k2, sl m, k2tog, k6 (8), k1f&b, sl m, k2, sl m, k1f&b, k6 (8), k2tog, sl m, k2, sl m, k2tog, k4, k1f&b, sl m, k2, sl m, k1.

Rep the last 2 rows 35 (37) more times, ending with a RS row—73 (77) rows completed above armhole; armhole measures about 8½ (9)" (21.5 [23] cm); piece measures about 19¼ (21)" (49 [53.5] cm) from joining row.

Shoulder Triangles

Cont as foll:

Row 1: (WS) BO 1 armhole edge st, then BO 2 sts of foll slip-stitch column, *knit to marked sts, sl m, sl 2 pwise wyf, sl m; rep from * 2 more times, knit to end—45 (53) sts rem.

Row 2: (RS) Sl 1 pwise wyb, k1f&b, k10 (14), k2tog, sl m, k2, sl m, ssk, k5 (7), k2tog to end at marked sts, place rem 20 (22) sts on holder, turn—23 (29) sts; 14 (18) sts in front edge triangle, 2 sts in slip-stitch column, 7 (9) sts from chevron.

Row 3: *Knit to marked sts, sl m, sl 2 pwise wyf, sl m, knit to end.

Row 4: Sl 1 pwise wyb, k1f&b, k10 (14), k2tog, sl m, k2, sl m, ssk, knit to last 2 sts, k2tog—2 sts dec'd in valley on chevron side of slip-stitch column; no change to sts in edge triangle at front edge.

Rep the last 2 rows 1 (2) more time(s), ending with a RS row—19 (23) sts rem; 14 (18) sts in front edge triangle, 2 sts in slip-stitch column, 3 sts in chevron section for both sizes. With WS facing, k3tog, then knit rem 16 (20) sts for right front neck and place 16 (20) sts just worked on holder for collar extension to be worked later—1 st rem. Break yarn and fasten off last st. Return 20 (22) held sts to needle and rejoin yarn with RS facing. Work as foll:

Row 1: (RS) BO 2 sts of slip-stitch column (1 st rem on right-hand needle after last BO), ssk, k4 (6), k2tog, sl m, k2, sl m, k2tog, k3, k2tog—14 (16) sts rem.

Row 2: Knit to marked sts, sl m, sl 2 pwise wyf, sl m, knit to end.

Row 3: Ssk, k3 (5), k2tog, sl m, k2, sl m, k2tog, k1, k2tog—10 (12) sts rem.

Row 4: K3, sl m, sl 2 pwise wyf, sl m, k2tog, k1 (0), [k3tog] 0 (1) time, k2tog—8 sts rem for both sizes.

With RS facing, [k2tog] 4 times, turn, [k2tog] 2 times, turn, k2tog—1 st rem. Break yarn and fasten off last st.

BACK

With A, work 5 Chevron Base Triangles, 2 with 7 rows and 18 sts, 2 with 9 (11) rows and 22 (26) sts, and 1 with 15 (17) rows and 34 (38) sts. Place all 5 triangles on needle with RS facing so that on the next RS row they will be worked in this order: 18-st triangle, 22 (26)-st triangle, 34 (38)-st triangle, 22 (26)-st triangle, 18-st triangle—114 (126) sts total. Join A with RS facing.

Joining row: K1 (edge st), k2tog, k4, k1f&b, sl m, k2, sl m, k1f&b, k4, k2tog, pm, k1 (last st of triangle), *k1 (first st of next triangle), pm, k2tog, k6 (8), k1f&b, sl m, k2, sl m, k1f&b, k6 (8), k2tog, pm, k1 (last st of triangle),* k1 (first st of next triangle), pm, k2tog, k12 (14), k1f&b, sl m, k2, sl m, k1f&b, k12 (14), k2tog, pm, k1 (last st of triangle); rep from * to * for second 22 (26)-st triangle, k1 (first st of rem triangle), pm, k2tog, k4, k1f&b, sl m, k2, sl m, k1f&b, k4, k2tog, k1 (edge st)—still 114 (126) sts.

Next row: (WS) *Knit to marked sts, sl m, sl 2 pwise wyf, sl m; rep from * 8 more times, knit to end.

Next row: (RS) K1 (edge st), *k2tog, knit to 1 st before marked sts, k1f&b, sl m, k2, sl m, k1f&b, knit to 2 sts before next marked sts, k2tog, sl m, k2, sl m; rep from * 3 more times, k2tog, knit to 1 st before marked sts, k1f&b, sl m, k2, sl m, k1f&b, knit to last 3 sts, k2tog, k1 (edge st).

Back

Rep the last 2 rows 44 (49) more times, then work 1 more WS row—92 (102) total rows from joining row (including joining row); piece measures about 10¾ (12)" (27.5 [30.5] cm) from joining row.

Shape Armholes

(RS) K1 (edge st), k2tog, k4, k1f&b, place first 7 of 8 sts just worked on holder for right back armhole (second st of k1f&b rem on needle), sl m, k2, sl m, k1f&b, k4, k2tog, sl m, k2, sl m, *k2tog, k6 (8), k1f&b, sl m, k2, sl m, k1f&b, k6 (8), k2tog, sl m, k2, sl m,* k2tog, k12 (14), k1f&b, sl m, k2, sl m, k1f&b, k12 (14), k2tog, sl m, k2, sl m; rep from * to * once more, k2tog, k4, k1f&b, sl m, k2, sl m, k1, place last 7 sts on holder for left back armhole—100 (112) sts.

Next row: (WS) K1 (armhole edge st), *sl m, sl 2 pwise wyf, sl m, knit to next marked sts; rep from * to last 3 sts, sl m, sl 2 pwise wyf, sl m, k1 (armhole edge st).

Next row: (RS) K1, *sl m, k2, sl m, k1f&b, knit to 2 sts before next 2 marked sts, k2tog, sl m, k2, sl m, k2tog, knit to 1 st before next 2 marked sts, k1f&b; rep from * 3 more times, sl m, k2, sl m, k1.

Rep the last 2 rows 35 (37) more times, ending with a RS row—73 (77) rows completed above armhole; armhole measures about 8½ (9)" (21.5 [23] cm); piece measures about 19¼ (21)" (49 [53.5] cm) from joining row.

Shoulder and Back Neck Triangles

Left Back Triangle

Row 1: (WS) BO 1 armhole edge st, then BO 2 sts of foll slip-stitch column (1 st rem on right-hand needle after BO), k6, sl m, sl 2 pwise wyf, sl m, k9 (11), place rem 79 (89) sts on holder—18 (20) sts rem.

Row 2: (RS) Ssk, k5 (7), k2tog, sl m, k2, sl m, ssk, k3, k2tog—14 (16) sts rem.

Row 3: Knit to marked sts, sl m, sl 2 pwise wyf, sl m, knit to end.

Row 4: Ssk, k3 (5), k2tog, sl m, k2, sl m, k2tog, k1, k2tog—10 (12) sts rem.

Row 5: K3, sl m, sl 2 pwise wyf, sl m, k2tog, k1 (0), [k3tog] 0 (1) time, k2tog—8 sts rem for both sizes.

With RS facing, [k2tog] 4 times, turn, [k2tog] 2 times, turn, k2tog—1 st rem. Break yarn and fasten off last st.

Center Back Triangles

With WS facing return next 30 (34) held sts to needle and join A—2 sts at each end should be slip-stitch column sts.

Row 1: (WS) BO 2 sts of slip-stitch column, knit to next marked sts, sl m, sl 2 pwise wyf, sl m, knit to end—28 (32) sts rem.

Row 2: (RS) BO 2 sts (1 st rem on right-hand needle after last BO), ssk, k10 (12), k2tog, sl m, k2, sl m, k2tog, k5 (7), k2tog—22 (26) sts rem.

Row 3: K7 (9), sl m, sl 2 pwise wyf, sl m, k2tog, k9 (11), ssk—20 (24) sts rem.

Row 4: Ssk, k7 (9), k2tog, sl m, k2, sl m, k2tog, k3 (5), k2tog—16 (20) sts rem.

Row 5: K5 (7), sl m, sl 2 pwise wyf, sl m, k2tog, k5 (7), ssk—14 (18) sts rem.

Row 6: Ssk, k3 (5), k2tog, sl m, k2, sl m, k2tog, k1 (3), k2tog—10 (14) sts rem.

Row 7: K1, k3tog 0 (1) time, k2 (1), sl m, sl 2 pwise wyf, sl m, k2tog, k1 (0), [k3tog] 0 (1) time, k2tog—8 sts rem for both sizes.

With RS facing, [k2tog] 4 times, turn, [k2tog] 2 times, turn, k2tog—1 st rem. Break yarn and fasten off last st. With WS facing, return next 28 (32) held sts to needle and join A—2 sts at end with WS facing should be slip-stitch column sts.

Row 1: (WS) Knit to marked sts, sl m, sl 2 pwise wyf, sl m, knit to end.

Row 2: (RS) BO 2 sts (1 st rem on right-hand needle after last BO), ssk, k4 (6), k2tog, sl m, k2, sl m, k2tog, k11 (13), k2tog—22 (26) sts rem.

Row 3: K2tog, k9 (11), k2tog, sl m, sl 2 pwise wyf, sl m, k7 (9) —20 (24) sts rem.

Row 4: Ssk, k3 (5), k2tog, sl m, k2, sl m, k2tog, k7 (9), k2tog—16 (20) sts rem.

Row 5: K2tog, k5 (7), k2tog, sl m, sl 2 pwise wyf, sl m, k5 (7)—14 (18) sts rem.

Row 6: Ssk, k1 (3), k2tog, sl m, k2, sl m, k2tog, k3 (5), k2tog—10 (14) sts rem.

Row 7: K2tog, k1 (0), k3tog 0 (1) time, k2tog, sl m, sl 2 pwise wyf, sl m, k1, [k3tog] 0 (1) time, k2 (1)—8 sts rem for both sizes.

With RS facing, [k2tog] 4 times, turn, [k2tog] 2 times, turn, k2tog—1 st rem. Break yarn and fasten off last st.

Right Back Triangle

With WS facing return rem 21 (23) held sts to needle and join A.

Row 1: (WS) K9 (11), sl m, sl 2 pwise wyf, sl m, k7, sl m, sl 2 pwise wyf, sl m, k1 (armhole edge st).

Row 2: (RS) BO 1 armhole edge st, then BO 2 sts of foll slip-stitch column (1 st rem on right-hand needle after BO), ssk, k2, k2tog, sl m, k2, sl m, k2tog, k5 (7), k2tog—14 (16) sts rem.

Row 3: Knit to marked sts, sl m, sl 2 pwise wyf, sl m, knit to end.

Row 4: Ssk, k1, k2tog, sl m, k2, sl m, k2tog, k3 (5), k2tog—10 (12) sts rem.

Row 5: K2tog, k1 (0), [k3tog] 0 (1) time, k2tog, sl m, sl 2 pwise wyf, sl m, k3—8 sts rem for both sizes.

With RS facing, [k2tog] 4 times, turn, [k2tog] 2 times, turn, k2tog—1 st rem. Break yarn and fasten off last st.

COLLAR

With A threaded on a tapestry needle, use the mattress st (see Glossary) to sew fronts to back at shoulders, matching slip-stitch columns. Steam-press carefully to measurements under a damp cloth, straightening shoulder lines, allowing lower edges of body to ripple gently. Return 16 (20) held right front collar sts to needles and rejoin A with RS facing. Mark slip stitch at center front edge (beg of RS rows) with waste yarn to indicate start of collar.

Next row: (RS) Sl 1 pwise wyb, k1f&b, k10 (14), k2tog, sl m, k2, pm, use the backward-loop method (see Glossary) to CO 1 st for seam—17 (21) sts.

Next row: (WS) K1 (seam st), sl m, sl 2 pwise wyf, sl m, knit to end.

Next row: (RS) Sl 1 pwise wyb, k1f&b, k10 (14), k2tog, sl m, k2, sl m, k1.

Rep the last 2 rows until slip-stitch front edge of collar measures 3 (3½)" (7.5 [9] cm) from marker at beg of collar, ending with a RS row. Fill in the collar valley as foll: On the next 7 (9) rows, k2tog, knit to last 2 sts, k2tog—2 sts dec'd each row; 3 sts rem when all rows have been completed; collar measures about the same length along both the slip-stitch front edge and the seam edge. With RS facing, k3tog, break yarn, and fasten off last st.

Return 16 (20) held left front collar sts to needles and rejoin A with RS facing. Mark slip stitch at center front edge (end of RS rows) with waste yarn to indicate start of collar.

Next row: (RS) Use the backward-loop method to CO 1 st for seam, k1 (new CO seam st), pm, k2, sl m, knit to end—17 (21) sts.

Next row: (WS) Sl 1 pwise wyf, k1f&b, k10 (14), k2tog, sl m, sl 2 pwise wyf, sl m, k1 (seam st).

Next row: (RS) K1, sl m, k2, sl m, knit to end.

Rep the last 2 rows until slip-stitch front edge of collar measures 3 (3½)" (7.5 [9] cm) from marker at beg of collar, ending with a RS row. Work last 7 (9) rows as for right collar—3 sts rem. With RS facing, k3tog, break yarn, and fasten off last st. Sew ends of collar extensions tog, then sew collar selvedge to back neck edge, easing to fit.

SLEEVES

With A, RS facing, and beg in corner of armhole notch, pick up and knit 42 (46) sts along armhole edge to shoulder seam, then 42 (46) sts along armhole edge from shoulder seam to other armhole notch—84 (92) sts total. Place 7 held armhole sts at each side on separate dpn.

Next row: (WS) Knit to last sleeve st, k2tog (last sleeve st tog with 1 st from armhole dpn)—1 armhole st has been joined.

Rep the last row 13 more times, ending with a RS row—all held armhole sts have been joined; piece measures about 1½" (3.8 cm) from pick-up row.

Next row: (WS) K1 (seam st), sl 1 pwise wyf, knit to last 2 sts, sl 1 pwise wyf, k1 (seam st).

Next row: (RS) Knit.

Rep the last 2 rows for patt and *at the same time* dec 1 st inside each slipped st every 0 (4) rows 0 (6) times, then every 6 rows 17 (15) times—50 sts rem for both sizes. Work even as established until sleeve measures 18½ (19½)" (47 [49.5] cm) from pick-up row, ending with a RS row. **Note:** Jacket shown photographed flat has 20¼" (52 cm) sleeves. BO all sts.

FINISHING

Block sleeves to measurements. With A threaded on a tapestry needle, use the mattress st to sew sleeve and side seams. Steam-press seams carefully. Weave in loose ends.

RAINBOW

The poncho that inspired this sweater served as a bed covering in my childhood room. I was drawn to the rich colors in the stripes. Later on, the juxtaposition of the natural alpaca and dyed colors caught my eye. The sweater is knitted using a slip-stitch technique that resembles twill fabric.

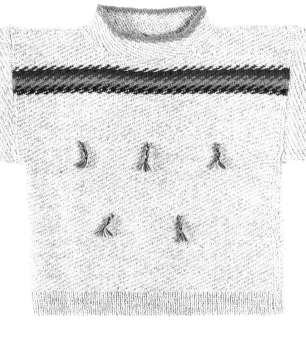

Finished Size
About 26 (29½, 33½)" (66 [75, 85] cm) chest circumference, to fit children's sizes 4 (6–8, 10). Sweater shown photographed flat measures 29½" (75 cm).

Yarn
About 125 (150, 200) grams of main color (A1) of laceweight (#0 Lace) yarn, 150 (200, 250) grams of a main color (A2), and small amounts of five (B1, B2, B3, B4, and B5) accent colors of fingering-weight (#1 Super Fine) yarn.

Shown here

Isager Wool 1 (100% wool; 340 yd [310 m]/50 g): #0 natural (A1), 3 (3, 4) skeins; and #2s light gray heather (A2), 3 (4, 4) skeins.

Isager Alpaca 2 (50% merino, 50% alpaca; 270 yd [247 m]/50 g): bottle green (B1; discontinued), lime green (B2; discontinued), gold (B3; discontinued), #014 orange (B4), and cerise (B5; discontinued, 1 skein each. **Note:** Substitute the colors of your choice for the discontinued colors.

Needles
Body and sleeves—size U.S. 4 (3.5 mm). *Ribbing*—size U.S. 2 (3.0 mm): straight and 16" (40 cm) circular (cir). Adjust needle size if necessary to obtain the correct gauge.

Notions
Stitch holders; removable markers or waste yarn; stitch marker; tapestry needle.

Gauge
34 stitches and 58 rows = 4" (10 cm) in herringbone pattern on larger needles using one strand each of A1 and A2 held together.

STITCH GUIDE

K1, P1 Rib

(worked over an odd number of sts)

Row 1: (RS) *K1, p1; rep from * to last st, k1.

Row 2: (WS) *P1, k1; rep from * to last st, p1.

Rep Rows 1 and 2 for patt.

Herringbone Pattern in Rows

(multiple of 4 sts + 2)

Note: Slip all sts as if to purl (pwise).

Row 1: (RS) K2 (selvedge sts), k1, *sl 2 with yarn in front (wyf), k2; rep from * to last 3 sts, sl 1 wyf, k2 (selvedge sts).

Row 2: K1, sl 1 wyf, *sl 2 with yarn in back (wyb), p2; rep from * to last 4 sts, sl 2 wyb, sl 1 wyf, k1.

Row 3: K2, sl 1 wyf, *k2, sl 2 wyf; rep from * to last 3 sts, k3.

Row 4: K1, sl 1 wyf, *p2, sl 2 wyb; rep from * to last 4 sts, p2, sl 1 wyf, k1.

Rep Rows 1–4 for patt.

Herringbone Pattern in Rounds

(multiple of 4 sts)

Note: Slip all sts as if to purl (pwise). When working in the round, the diagonal slip-stitch lines will slant in the opposite direction from the pattern worked in rows.

Rnd 1: K1, *sl 2 wyf, k2; rep from * to last 3 sts, sl 2 wyf, k1.

Rnd 2: *K2, sl 2 wyf; rep from *.

Rnd 3: Sl 1 wyf, *k2, sl 2 wyf; rep from * to last 3 sts, k2, sl 1 wyf.

Rnd 4: *Sl 2 wyf, k2; rep from *.

Rep Rnds 1–4 for patt.

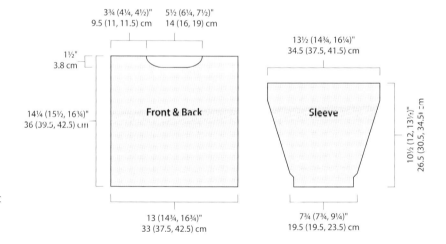

3¾ (4¼, 4½)"
9.5 (11, 11.5) cm

5½ (6¼, 7½)"
14 (16, 19) cm

13½ (14¾, 16¼)"
34.5 (37.5, 41.5) cm

1½"
3.8 cm

14¼ (15½, 16¾)"
36 (39.5, 42.5) cm

Front & Back

Sleeve

10½ (12, 13½)"
26.5 (30.5, 34.5) cm

13 (14¾, 16¾)"
33 (37.5, 42.5) cm

7¾ (7¾, 9¼)"
19.5 (19.5, 23.5) cm

NOTE

- Use one strand each of A1 and A2 held together throughout for main color. Use two strands held together for each of accent colors B1, B2, B3, B4, and B5.

BACK

With 1 strand each of A1 and A2 held tog and smaller needles, CO 109 (125, 141) sts. Work in k1, p1 rib (see Stitch Guide) for 1¼ (1½, 1¾)" (3.2 [3.8, 4.5] cm), beg and ending with WS Row 2, and inc 1 st in last row—110 (126, 142) sts. Change to larger needles. Work herringbone patt in rows (see Stitch Guide) until piece measures 10¾ (12, 13¼)" (27.5 [30.5, 33.5] cm) from CO, ending with Row 4 of patt.

Next 20 rows: Cont in patt, work 4 rows each with colors B1, B2, B3, B4, and B5, using 2 strands held tog for each accent color.

Change to 1 strand each of A1 and A2 held tog again, and work even in patt until piece measures 14¼ (15½, 16¾)" (36 [39.5, 42.5] cm) from CO, ending with a WS row. Place 31 (35, 39) sts at each side on separate holders for shoulders, and place center 48 (56, 64) sts on a third holder for back neck.

FRONT

Work as for back until piece measures ¾" (2 cm) above last accent color row, ending with a WS row—110 (126, 142) sts; piece measures about 12¾ (14, 15¼)" (32.5 [35.5, 38.5] cm) from CO.

Shape Neck

(RS) Work 40 (45, 50) sts in patt, place next 30 (36, 42) center front sts on holder, join new balls of A1 and A2, work in patt to end—40 (45, 50) sts at each side. Working each side separately, cont in patt and

Practice the stitch patterns and color sequence on a gauge swatch.

dec 1 st at each side of neck (2 sts in from the neck edge) every row 9 (10, 11) times—31 (35, 39) sts rem at each side. Work even in patt until piece measures 14¼ (15½, 16¾)" (36 [39.5, 42.5] cm) from CO, ending with a WS row. Place sts at each side on separate holders for shoulders.

SLEEVES

With 1 strand each of A1 and A2 held tog and smaller needles, CO 49 (53, 57) sts. Work in k1, p1

Back

rib for 1¼ (1½, 2)" (3.2 [3.8, 5] cm), beg and ending with WS Row 2, and inc 17 (13, 21) sts evenly spaced in last row—66 (66, 78) sts. Change to larger needles. Work herringbone patt in rows and *at the same time* inc 1 st at each end of needle (2 sts in from the edge) every 4th row 24 (30, 30) times, working new sts into patt—114 (126, 138) sts. Work even in patt until piece measures 10½ (12, 13½)" (26.5 [30.5, 34.5] cm) from CO, ending with a WS row. BO all sts.

FINISHING

Carefully steam-press pieces to measurements on WS under a damp cloth. Join back to front at shoulders using the three-needle bind-off method (see Glossary).

Neckband

With 1 strand each of A1 and A2 held tog and cir needle in smaller size, knit across 48 (56, 64) held back neck sts, pick up and knit 15 (14, 15) sts along left front neck, knit across 30 (36, 42) held sts at center front, then pick up and knit 15 (14, 15) sts along right front neck—108 (120, 136) sts total. Place marker (pm) and join for working in rnds. Work herringbone patt in rnds (see Stitch Guide) until neckband measures ¾ (1¼, 1½)" (2 [3.2, 3.8] cm) from pick-up rnd, ending with Rnd 4 of patt. Change to 2 strands held tog in the contrast color of your choice (B3 gold shown). Work Rnds 1–4 of patt once more—neckband measures about 1 (1½, 1¾)" (2.5 [3.8, 4.5] cm) from pick-up rnd. BO all sts loosely with same accent color.

Measure down 6¾ (7¼, 8)" (17 [18.5, 20.5] cm) from shoulder joins along each side of front and back and mark positions with removable markers or waste yarn. With 1 strand each of A1 and A2 threaded on a tapestry needle, use the mattress st (see Glossary) to sew BO edges of sleeves between markers. With A1 and A2 threaded on a tapestry needle, use the mattress st to sew sleeve and side seams, working with a 1-stitch seam allowance so the slipped sts located 1 st in from the edges draw together on each side of the seams for a decorative effect. Weave in loose ends.

Braids (optional)

With removable markers or waste yarn, mark positions for 5 braids on back: The upper 3 braids about 3" (7.5 cm) below first accent color row and evenly spaced horizontally to divide the back width into quarters, and the lower 2 braids about 4" (10 cm) below the upper braids and centered between each pair of upper braids. Mark positions for 5 braids on the front in the same manner. Make 10 braids as foll: Cut 6 strands of yarn in random colors each about 6" (15 cm) long. Thread a 6-strand bundle on a tapestry needle and anchor it at one of the marked positions by taking a small stitch through the fabric. Pull the ends of the strands even and divide them into 3 groups of 4 strands each. Braid the groups for about ¾" (2 cm), then use one strand to wrap the end of the braid tightly as shown. Secure the end of the wrapping strand and trim the ends of the braid to about ⅝" (1.5 cm) long. Make and attach 9 more braids in the same manner.

The braids on this sweater mimic the colorful braids added to a woven blanket.

LLAMA

Llamas, cats, birds, and many other animals, as well as labyrinth motifs, are often found in the Latin American designs. Many of my knitwear designs have been inspired by the animal and labyrinth motifs on Peruvian caps.

Finished Size

About 32¼ (37¼, 37¼, 43)" (82 [94.5, 94.5, 109] cm) bust/chest circumference, to fit sizes child 8–10 (child 10–12, adult small, adult medium). Sweater shown photographed flat measures 37¼" (94.5 cm) in child 10–12 length (see Notes on page 114).

Yarn

About 100 (150, 175, 200) grams of a medium color (A), 100 (125, 150, 175) grams of a dark color (B), and 50 (60, 80, 100) grams of a light color (C) of fingering-weight (#1 Super Fine) yarn.

Shown here

Isager Alpaca 2 (50% merino, 50% alpaca; 270 yd [247 m]/50 g): #284 light brown heather (A), 2 (3, 3, 4) skeins; #402 charcoal (B), 2 (3, 3, 4) skeins; and #2105 light gray heather (C), 1 (2, 2, 2) skein(s).

Needles

Body and sleeves—size U.S. 4 (3.5 mm) 16" and 24" (40 and 60 cm) circular (cir) and set of 4 or 5 double-pointed (dpn). *Ribbing and neckband*—size U.S. 2 (3.0 mm) one 24" (60 cm), two 16" (40 cm) cir and set of 4 or 5 dpn. Adjust needle size if necessary to obtain the correct gauge.

Notions

Stitch holders; marker (m); removable markers or waste yarn; . tapestry needle; sharp-point sewing needle or sewing machine; contrasting basting thread; matching sewing thread.

Gauge

32 stitches and 36½ rows = 4" (10 cm) in solid-color stockinette-stitch and colorwork patterns from charts on larger needles.

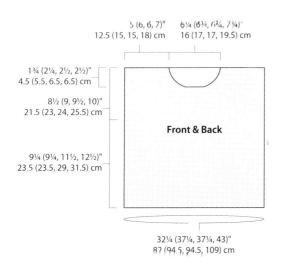

5 (6, 6, 7)"
12.5 (15, 15, 18) cm

6¼ (6¾, 6¾, 7¼)"
16 (17, 17, 19.5) cm

1¾ (2¼, 2½, 2½)"
4.5 (5.5, 6.5, 6.5) cm

8½ (9, 9½, 10)"
21.5 (23, 24, 25.5) cm

Front & Back

9¼ (9¼, 11½, 12½)"
23.5 (23.5, 29, 31.5) cm

32¼ (37¼, 37¼, 43)"
82 (94.5, 94.5, 109) cm

17 (18, 19, 20)"
43 (45.5, 48.5, 51) cm

Sleeve

15½ (16, 18, 19)"
39.5 (40.5, 45.5, 48.5) cm

8¼ (8¼, 8¾, 9¼)"
21 (21, 22, 23.5) cm

NOTES

■ This sweater is worked in stranded two-color knitting (see page 26).

■ The body is worked in the round to the start of the neck shaping with steeks for the armhole openings. The neck shaping is worked back and forth in rows to the shoulders. The sleeves are worked in the round with facings at the upper edges to cover the raw edges of the steeked armhole openings.

■ The second and third sizes, child 10–12 and adult small, both have the same number of stitches in the body (and therefore the same chest circumference), but the adult's version has a longer body and longer sleeves than the child's version.

BODY

With A and longer cir needle in smaller size, CO 256 (296, 296, 340) sts. Place marker (pm) and join for working in rnds; rnd beg at start of back sts.

Next rnd: *K2, p2; rep from *.

Work sts as they appear (knit the knits and purl the purls) until piece measures 1¾" (4.5 cm). Change to longer cir needle in larger size.

Rnd 1: With A, knit inc 2 (2, 2, 4) sts evenly spaced—258 (298, 298, 344) sts.

Rnds 2–4: Knit 1 rnd each of C, B, and A.

Rnd 5: Establish patt from Rnd 1 of Labyrinth chart as foll: *Work 1 st before patt rep box, rep 14-st patt 9 (10, 10, 12) times, work 2 (8, 8, 3) sts after patt rep box,* pm for left side; rep from * to * once more for

This hat inspired the llama design in the sweater.

front—129 (149, 149, 172) sts each for back and front.

Rnds 6–13: Work Rnds 2–9 of Labyrinth chart as established.

Rnds 14–16: Knit 1 rnd each of A, B, and C.

Rnd 17: Using A for background color (blank squares) and B for llama patt color (Xs), establish patt from Rnd 1 of Llama chart as foll: *Work 2 sts before patt rep box, work 64-st rep 1 (2, 2, 2) time(s), work first 63 (0, 0, 42) sts of patt rep box, then work 0 (19, 19, 0) sts after patt rep box; rep from * once more for front.

Rnds 18–37: Using A for background and B for llama patt color, work Rnds 2–21 of Llama chart as established.

Rnds 38–40: Knit 1 rnd each of B, C, and A.

Rnds 41–49: Rep Rnds 5–13 for Labyrinth chart, omitting pm because left side m is already in place.

Rnds 50–52: Knit 1 rnd each of B, C, and A.

Rnd 53: Using B for background color and C for llama patt color, establish patt from Rnd 1 of Llama chart as for Rnd 17.

Rnds 54–68 (68, 90, 98): Using B for background color and C for llama patt color, work Rnd 2–Rnd 16 (16, 38, 42) of Llama chart once, then work 0 (0, 0, 4) more rnds to end with Rnd 16 (16, 38, 4)—piece measures about 9¼ (9¼, 11½, 12½)" (23.5 [23.5, 29, 31.5] cm) from CO.

Armhole Steeks

Rnd 69 (69, 91, 99): CO 3 sts in alternating colors for right armhole steek, pm, work Rnd 17 (17, 39, 5) as established to end of back sts, slip side m, CO 3 sts in alternating colors for left armhole steek, pm, work Rnd 17 (17, 39, 5) as established to end of front sts—264 (304, 304, 350) sts; 129 (149, 149, 172) sts each for back and front; 3 steek sts at each armhole.

On the foll rnds, work the 3 steek sts at each side in a solid color, 1×1 checkerboard patt, or stripes, as you prefer in order to distinguish them from the patt sts.

Rnd 70 (70, 92, 100) to Rnd 115: Work 46 (46, 24, 16) more rnds in patt from Llama chart, ending with Rnd 21 of chart for all sizes.

Rnds 116–118: Knit 1 rnd each of A, C, and B.

Half Flower

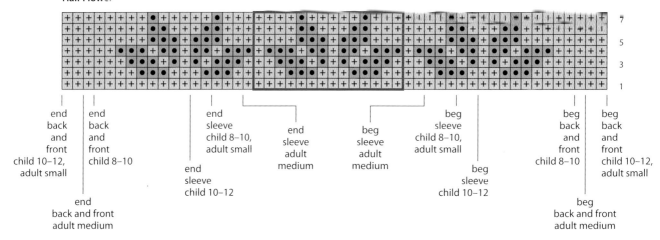

end
back
and
front
child 10–12,
adult small

end
back
and
front
child 8–10

end
back and front
adult medium

end
sleeve
child 10–12

end
sleeve
child 8–10,
adult small

end
sleeve
adult
medium

beg
sleeve
adult
medium

beg
sleeve
child 10–12

beg
sleeve
child 8–10,
adult small

beg
back
and
front
child 8–10

beg
back and front
adult medium

beg
back
and
front
child 10–12,
adult small

7
5
3
1

Sleeve

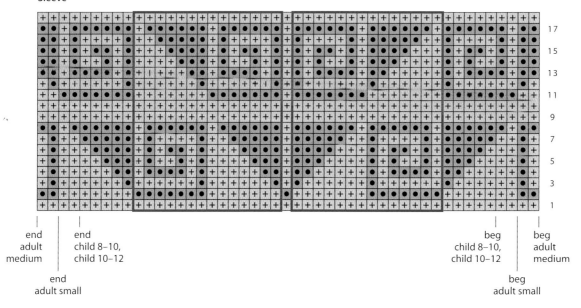

end
adult
medium

end
adult small

end
child 8–10,
child 10–12

beg
child 8–10,
child 10–12

beg
adult small

beg
adult
medium

17
15
13
11
9
7
5
3
1

Llama

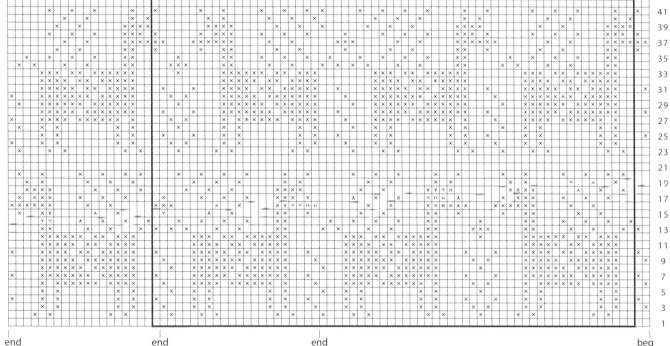

41
39
37
35
33
31
29
27
25
23
21
19
17
15
13
11
9
7
5
3
1

end
back and front
child 10–12,
adult small

end
back and front
child 8–10

end
back and front
adult medium

beg
back and front
all sizes

Labyrinth

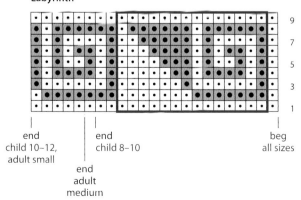

9
7
5
3
1

end
child 10–12,
adult small

end
adult
medium

end
child 8–10

beg
all sizes

+	A
•	B
·	C

	A or B (see instructions)
×	B or C (see instructions)
	pattern repeat

Rnds 119–127: Cont steek sts, work Labyrinth chart on back and front sts as for Rnds 41–49.

Rnds 128–130: Knit 1 rnd each of B, A, and C, inc 0 (0, 0, 1) st on both back and front in last rnd—264 (304, 304, 352) sts; 129 (149, 149, 173) sts each for back and front; 3 steek sts at each armhole; piece measures about 16" (40.5 cm) from CO.

Shape Neck

Child Sizes 8–10 (10–12) Only
With removable markers or waste yarn, mark 21 sts at center front—54 (64) front sts on each side of marked sts.

Rnd 131: Work 3 steek sts, work Rnd 1 of Half Flower chart to end of back sts, beg and ending where indicated for your size, work 3 steek sts, work Rnd 1 of Half Flower chart to marked center sts, join new yarn and BO center 21 sts, cont Half Flower chart to end—54 (64) front sts rem at each side. Break yarn.

Row 132: (WS) Sl sts as if to purl without working them until you reach the BO gap at center front. Turn work so WS is facing and rejoin yarns at left neck edge. BO 4 sts at left neck edge, then work Row 2 of Half Flower chart as a WS row to left armhole steek, work 3 steek sts, work in chart patt across back sts, work 3 right armhole steek sts, work in patt across right front neck sts to end at center front BO gap. Rows now beg and end at neck edges.

Row 133: BO 4 sts at right neck edge, work Row 3 of chart and steeks as established to end—50 (60) front sts at each side.

Rows 134–137: Work Rows 4–7 of chart with steeks as established and *at the same time* at each neck edge, BO 3 sts once, then BO 2 sts once —45 (55) front sts at each side.

Cont in St st with A, at each neck edge, BO 2 sts 2 (3) times, then BO 1 st 1 time—215 (251) sts rem; 40 (48) front sts at each side; 129 (149) back sts; 3 steek sts at each armhole. Work even in St st with A until piece measures 17¾ (18¼)" (45 [46.5] cm) from CO or desired length to shoulders. Place steek, back, and front sts on separate holders.

Size (adult small, adult medium) Only
Rnds 131–137: Cont steek sts as established, work Rnds 1–7 of Half Flower chart on back and front, beg and ending where indicated for your size— piece measures about 16¾" (42.5 cm) from CO.

Cont in St st with A until piece measures (18½, 20)" ([47, 51] cm) from CO. With removable markers or waste yarn, mark 21 sts at center front—(64, 76) front sts on each side of marked sts.

Next rnd: With A, work 3 steek sts, knit to end of back sts, work 3 steek sts, knit to marked center sts, join new yarn and BO center 21 sts, knit to end—(64, 76) front sts rem at each side. Break yarn.

Sl sts as if to purl without working them until you reach the BO gap at center front. Turn work so WS is facing, rejoin A at left neck edge. With WS facing, BO 4 sts at left neck edge, purl to end; rows now beg and end at neck edges. With RS facing, BO 4 sts at right neck edge, knit to end—(60, 72) front sts at each side. Cont in St st with A, at each neck edge BO 3 sts (1, 2) time(s), then BO 2 sts 4 times, then BO 1 st (1, 2) time(s)—(251, 291) sts rem; (48, 56) front sts at each side; (149, 173) back sts; 3 steek sts at each armhole. Work even in St st with A until piece measures (21, 22½)" ([53.5, 57] cm) from CO, or desired length to shoulders. Place steek, back, and front sts on separate holders.

Back

SLEEVES

With A and smaller dpn, CO 64 (64, 68, 72) sts. Pm and join for working in rnds. *K2, p2; rep from *. Work sts as they appear until piece measures 1¾" (4.5 cm). Change to larger dpn. Knit 1 rnd each of A, B, A, C, inc 3 sts evenly spaced in last rnd—67 (67, 71, 75) sts.

Set-up rnd: Establish patt from Rnd 1 of Sleeve chart as foll: Work 5 (5, 7, 9) sts before first patt rep box, work first 14-st patt rep box 2 times, work 1 center st, work second 14-st patt rep box 2 times, work 5 (5, 7, 9) sts after second patt rep box.

Note: Incs are worked at same time as chart patt; read the next sections all the way through before proceeding.

Beg on the next rnd, inc 1 st on each side of end-of-rnd m every 4 rnds 17 (11, 20, 14) times, then every 3 rnds 10 (18, 12, 20) times, working new sts into chart patt, and changing to shorter cir needle in larger size when there are too many sts to fit on dpn—121 (125, 135, 143) sts. *At the same time* work Rnds 2–18 of chart once, then rep Rnds 1–18 four (four (five, five) more times, then work Rnds 1–9 once more—99 (99, 117, 117) chart rnds completed; piece measures about 13 (13, 15, 15)" (33 [33, 38, 38] cm) from CO. Knit 1 rnd each of B and C. Work Rnds 1–7 of Half Flower chart, beg and ending where indicated for your size and *at the same time* inc 1 st at each side on Rnds 2 and 6, working new sts into chart patt—125 (129, 139, 147) sts; piece measures about 14 (14, 16, 16)"

(35.5 [35.5, 40.5, 40.5] cm) from CO. Cont in St st with A, inc 1 st each side of m every other rnd 6 (7, 7, 7) times—137 (143, 153, 161) sts. Work even in St st until sleeve measures 15½ (16, 18, 19)" (39.5 [40.5, 45.5, 48.5] cm) from CO or desired length. With A, purl 1 rnd, then work in St st for ⅝" (1.5 cm) for armhole facing. BO all sts.

FINISHING

Carefully steam-press pieces to measurements under a damp cloth. **Note:** Armhole facings are not shown on schematic.

Steeks

Baste a line of contrasting thread along the center of each 3-st steek. With sewing machine or by hand, sew a line of small straight stitches one stitch away on both sides of the basting line. Sew over the same two lines of stitching again. Carefully cut open each armhole along the basting line.

Neckband

Join 40 (48, 48, 56) shoulder sts of back to front using the three-needle bind-off method (see Glossary)—49 (53, 53, 61) sts rem at center back neck. With A, shorter cir needle in smaller size, and RS facing, knit across 49 (53, 53, 61) held back neck sts, pick up and knit 17 (21, 25, 23) sts along left front neck, 21 sts across center front, and 17 (21, 25, 23) sts along right front neck—104 (110, 111, 128) sts total. Pm and join for working in rnds.

Rnds 1–6: *K2 with B, k2 with C; rep from *.

Rnd 7: (welt rnd) With WS facing, slip the second shorter cir needle in smaller size into each purl bump of the neckband pick-up rnd; these loops are just picked up and placed on the needle, not picked up and knitted—104 (116, 124, 128) picked-up loops on second cir needle. Hold cir needles tog and parallel with RS of neckband facing, live sts of neckband on needle in front (working needle), and picked-up loops on needle in back. With A, *insert right-hand tip of working needle into first st on both needles and k2tog (1 st from each needle); rep from * to complete welt—104 (116, 124, 128) sts total on working needle; no picked-up loops rem.

Rnds 8–19: With A, *k2, p2; rep from *.

Rnd 20: Change to B and work in established rib.

BO all sts in rib patt with B.

Sew sleeves into armholes, sewing between the first patt st and outermost steek st on the body, and sewing just below the purled rnd at the top of the sleeve so purled sleeve sts do not show on RS of garment. Sew facings at top of sleeves invisibly on WS to conceal cut edges of steeks.

Weave in loose ends.

THE INCAS AND LLAMAS

The Incas—a culture and a people—have roots in small provincial towns, each with a unique language and history that is fascinating to outsiders like me.

We've learned that the Incas were a democratic people who never allowed their Indian culture to be destroyed by conquerors. Their social and work cultures are as strong today as when they built astounding stone structures that cannot be replicated with today's advanced technology.

Llamas, cats, birds, and many other animals as well as labyrinth motifs are often found in Latin American textiles and pottery. Llama, Stars, Birds, and Butterflies, Inca Jacket, and Indiana were all inspired by a Peruvian cap decorated with animal motifs and labyrinth patterns.

The Incas left their mark on the magnificent landscape.

STARS, BIRDS, AND BUTTERFLIES

This simple boatneck pullover is trimmed with an array of star, bird, and butterfly motifs. The back is intentionally 1½" (3.8 cm) longer than the front.

Finished Size
About 36½ (40¾, 45¼, 49½)" (92.5 [103.5, 115, 125.5] cm) bust circumference. Sweater shown photographed flat measures 45¼" (115 cm).

Yarn
About 150 (175, 200, 225) grams of a medium main color (A), 150 (175, 200, 225) grams of a dark second color (B), 20 (30, 40, 50) grams of a light color (C), 50 (55, 60, 65) grams of a bright facing and welt color (D), and small amounts of two accent colors (D and E) of fingering-weight (#1 Super Fine) yarn.

Shown here
Isager Wool 1 (100% wool; 340 yd [310 m]/50 g): #52s plum heather (A), 3 (4, 4, 5) skeins.

Isager Alpaca 2 (50% merino, 50% alpaca; 270 yd [247 m]/50 g): #011 steel blue (B), 3 (4, 4, 5) skeins; #284 light brown heather (C), 1 skein; periwinkle (D; discontinued), 1 (2, 2, 2) skeins; and #014

orange (E) and wine (F; discontinued), less than 1 skein each.

Note: Substitute the colors of your choice for the discontinued colors.

Needles
Body and sleeves—size U.S. 2 (3 mm): 16" and 24" (40 and 60 cm) circular and set of 4 or 5 double-pointed (dpn). *Facings and welts*— size U.S. 1 (2.5 mm): two 24" (60 cm) cir. Adjust needle size if necessary to obtain the correct gauge.

Notions
Stitch holders; markers (m); removable markers or waste yarn; tapestry needle; sharp-point sewing needle or sewing machine; contrasting basting thread; matching sewing thread.

Gauge
29 stitches and 34½ rows = 4" (10 cm) in stockinette-stitch colorwork patterns from charts on larger needles; 30 stitches and 52 rows = 4" (10 cm) in Diagonal Brocade pattern on larger needles.

STITCH GUIDE

Diagonal Brocade

(multiple of 8 sts + 6)

Row 1: (RS) K1 (selvedge st), *k4, p4; rep from * to last 5 sts, k4, k1 (selvedge st).

Row 2: (WS) K2, *p4, k4; rep from * to last 4 sts, p3, k1.

Row 3: K3, *p4, k4; rep from * to last 3 sts, p2, k1.

Row 4: *K4, p4; rep from * to last 6 sts, k4, p1, k1.

Row 5: K1, *p4, k4; rep from * to last 5 sts, p4, k1.

Row 6: K1, p1, *k4, p4; rep from * to last 4 sts, k4.

Row 7: K1, p2, *k4, p4; rep from * to last 3 sts, k3.

Row 8: K1, p3, *k4, p4; rep from * to last 2 sts, k2.

Rep Rows 1–8 for patt.

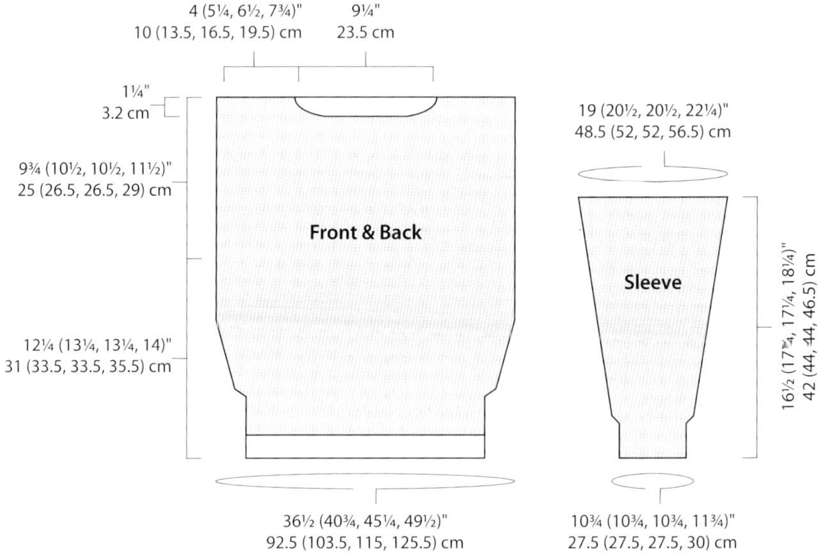
4 (5¼, 6½, 7¾)"
10 (13.5, 16.5, 19.5) cm
9¼"
23.5 cm
1¼"
3.2 cm
9¾ (10½, 10½, 11½)"
25 (26.5, 26.5, 29) cm
Front & Back
12¼ (13¼, 13¼, 14)"
31 (33.5, 33.5, 35.5) cm
36½ (40¾, 45¼, 49½)"
92.5 (103.5, 115, 125.5) cm
19 (20½, 20½, 22¼)"
48.5 (52, 52, 56.5) cm
Sleeve
16½ (17¼, 17¼, 18¼)"
42 (44, 44, 46.5) cm
10¾ (10¾, 10¾, 11¾)"
27.5 (27.5, 27.5, 30) cm

NOTES

- This sweater is worked in stranded two-color knitting (see page 26).
- The lower borders of the front and back are worked separately, back and forth in rows, with the back border 1½" (3.8 cm) longer than the front border. The body is then worked in the round to the start of the neck shaping with steeks for the armhole openings. The front neck shaping is worked back and forth in short-rows to the base of the neckband, then the patterned boat neckband is worked in the round on all stitches to the shoulders. The sleeves are worked in the round with facings at the upper edges to cover the raw edges of the steeked armhole openings.

BODY

Lower Front Border

With D and smaller cir needle, CO 102 (118, 126, 142) sts. Knitting the first and last st of every row for selvedge sts, work the center 100 (116, 124, 140) sts in St st until piece measures 2½" (6.5 cm) from CO, ending with a RS row. Change to longer cir needle in larger size. With B, knit 1 WS row for turning ridge. With B, work diagonal brocade patt (see Stitch Guide) until piece measures 2½" (6.5 cm) from turning ridge, ending with a WS row. Break yarn and place sts on holder.

Lower Back Border

Work same as front border until facing with D measures 4" (10 cm) from CO, ending with a RS row. Change to larger cir needle. With B, knit 1 WS row for turning ridge. Work as for front border until piece measures 4" (10 cm) from turning ridge, ending with a WS row. Do not break yarn.

Join Borders

With RS facing and using B attached to back border sts on larger cir, knit across 102 (118, 126, 142) back border sts, place marker (pm) for left side, then knit across 102 (118, 126, 142) held front border sts. Place marker (pm) and join for working in rnds—204 (236, 252, 284) sts; rnd beg at start of back sts. With B, knit 1 rnd inc 8 (8, 16, 16) sts evenly spaced on each back and front—220 (252, 284, 316) sts; 110 (126, 142, 158) sts each for back and front. Establish patt from Rnd 1 of Body and Sleeves chart as

foll: *Work 3 sts before patt rep box, rep 8-st patt 13 (15, 17, 19) times, work 3 sts after patt rep box,* sl side m; rep from * to * once more for front sts; motif placement is deliberately not symmetrical. Cont in patt from chart and *at the same time* inc 1 st on each side of each m (4 sts total inc'd) every 4 rnds 11 times, working new sts into chart patt—264 (296, 328, 360) sts; 132 (148, 164, 180) sts each for back and front; piece measures about 9¼" (23.5 cm) from lower back turning ridge and 1½" (3.8 cm) less from lower front turning ridge. Work even in patt until 70 (77, 77, 84) chart rows have been completed, ending with Rnd 14 (7, 7, 14) of chart—piece measures about 12¼ (13¼, 13¼, 14)" (31 [33.5, 33.5, 35.5] cm) from lower back turning ridge.

Armhole Steeks

Use the backward-loop method (see Glossary) to CO 3 sts for right armhole steek, pm, work Rnd 1 (8, 8, 1) as established to end of back sts, slip side m, CO 3 sts for left armhole steek, pm, work Rnd 1 (8, 8, 1) as established to end of front sts—270 (302, 334, 366) sts; 132 (148, 164, 180) sts each for back and front; 3 steek sts at each armhole. On the foll rnds, work the 3 steek sts at each side in a solid color, 1×1 checkerboard patt, or stripes, as you prefer in order to distinguish them from the patt sts. Cont in established patt until 120 (134, 134, 148) chart rnds have been completed from beg, ending with Rnd 8 of patt—armholes measure about 5¾ (6½, 6½, 7½)" (14.5 [16.5, 16.5, 19] cm). Break yarns.

Shape Neck

Mark center 40 front sts with removable markers—46 (54, 62, 70) front sts on each side of marked sts. Slip sts as if to purl (pwise) without working them to m at end of 40 marked center front sts (right neck edge), and rejoin yarn. (**Note:** While shaping neck, work chart patt in rows until Row 14 has been completed, then work rem rows in St st with A. Do not work any partial plus sign motifs from chart; if you think there will not be enough sts or rows to finish a complete motif, work the sts with A instead.) Working chart patt back and forth in rows (knit on odd-numbered RS rows, purl on even-numbered WS rows), shape front neck using short-rows as foll:

Short-row 1: (RS) Work in patt to end of right front, across back and steeks, and across left front neck to end at marked center sts (left neck edge), yo with A, turn. Rows now beg and end on each side of front neck.

Short-row 2: (WS) Work in patt to end of left front, across back and steeks, and across right front neck to end at marked center sts (right neck edge), yo with A, turn.

Short-rows 3–6: Work in patt to 5 sts before previous turning point, yo with A, turn; Short-row 6 completes Row 14 of chart; cont from here in St st with A.

Short-rows 7 and 8: Work to 2 sts before previous turning point, yo with A, turn.

Short-rows 9 and 10: Work to 1 st before previous turning point, yo with A, turn—66 center sts (not counting yarnovers) in shaped section; 33 (41, 49, 57) front sts rem on each side of neck shaping.

Next rnd: K33 (41, 49, 57) to end of right front neck, then knit 1 rnd across all sts to end just before right armhole steek sts, working yarnovers along left neck edge tog with the sts after them as k2tog, and working yarnovers along the right neck edge tog with the sts before them as ssk (see Glossary).

Knit 1 rnd with E. Knit 1 rnd with F, dec 8 (3, 0, 2) sts evenly spaced each in back and front—254 (296, 334, 362) sts; 124 (145, 164, 178) sts each for back and front; 3 steek sts at each armhole; armholes measure about 7¼ (8, 8, 9)" (18.5 [20.5, 20.5, 23] cm) at shoulders and about 1¼" (3.2 cm) less at center front.

Neckband

Change to smaller cir needle and knit 7 rnds with D. With WS facing, slip the second smaller cir needle into each purl bump along the first rnd of D; these loops are just picked-up and placed on the needle, not picked up and knitted—254 (296, 334, 362) picked-up loops on second cir needle. Hold cir needles tog and parallel with RS facing, live sts on front needle, and picked up loops on back needle. Using C, *insert right-hand tip of larger needle into first st on both smaller needles and k2tog (1 st from each needle); rep from * to end—254 (296, 334, 362) sts on larger working needle; all picked-up loops have been joined. Establish patt from Rnd 1 of Neckband chart as foll: *Work 3 steek sts, work 83-st patt rep 1 (1, 1, 2) time(s), then

☐	A
☒	B
⊡	C
☐	pattern repeat

Body and Sleeves

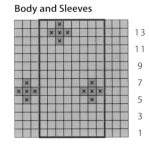

Neckband

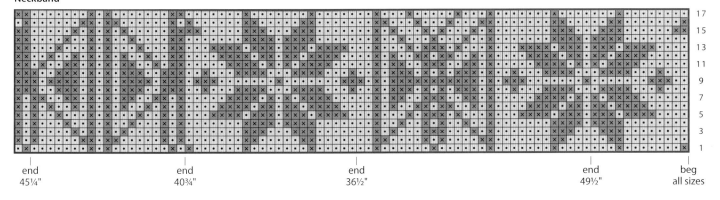

end	end	end	end	beg
45¼"	40¾"	36½"	49½"	all sizes

work first 41 (62, 81, 12) sts of rep once more to end where indicated for your size; rep from * once more for front. **Note:** The placement of the motifs is deliberately not symmetrical. Cont in established patt until Rnd 17 of chart has been completed. Knit 1 rnd with C. Change to smaller cir needle and knit 7 rnds with D. With WS facing, slip the second smaller cir needle into each purl bump along the first rnd of D as before. Using D and larger cir needle, join picked-up loops as for first neckband welt—armholes measure about 9¾ (10½, 10½, 11½)" (25 [26.5, 26.5, 29] cm)

at shoulder edges of second welt joining rnd. BO all sts with D and larger cir needle.

SLEEVES

Cuff

With D and smaller cir needle, CO 62 (62, 62, 70) sts. Knitting the first and last st of every row for selvedge sts, work the center 60 (60, 60, 68) sts in St st until piece measures 2¼" (5.5 cm) from CO, ending with a RS row. Change to shorter cir needle

dpn—138 (148, 148, 162) sts. Knit 2 rnds with A, knit 1 rnd with E, knit 1 rnd with F—piece measures about 16½ (17¼, 17¼, 18¼)" (42 [44, 44, 46.5] cm) from turning ridge. With A, purl 1 rnd, then work in St st for ⅝" (1.5 cm) for armhole facing. BO all sts.

FINISHING

Carefully steam-press pieces to measurements under a damp cloth, smoothing neckband tucks upward. **Note:** The cuff is shown in the round on the schematic even though it is worked in rows; lower border, cuff, and armhole facings are not shown on schematic.

Steeks

Baste a line of contrasting thread along the center of each 3-st steek. With sewing machine or by hand, sew a line of small straight stitches one stitch away on each side of the basting line. Sew over the same two lines of stitching again. Carefully cut open each armhole along the basting line.

Turn lower border and cuff facings to WS along turning ridges and use A threaded on a tapestry needle to sew facings in place on WS. With B threaded on a tapestry needle, use the mattress st (see Glossary) to close openings on each side of lower borders, leaving borders unconnected for side slits. Close openings on each side of cuff in the same manner without sewing cuff into a rnd to leave a split in the cuff. With D threaded on a tapestry needle, sew 29 (39, 48, 56) shoulder sts tog at each side along joining rnd of upper neckband facing, leaving center 66 (67, 68, 66)

Back

in larger size. With B, knit 1 WS row for turning ridge. With B, work diagonal brocade patt until piece measures 2¼" (5.5 cm) from turning ridge, ending with a WS row. Transfer sts to dpn, pm, and join for working in rnds. With A, knit 1 rnd, inc 16 sts evenly spaced—78 (78, 78, 86) sts. Establish patt from Rnd 1 of Body and Sleeves chart as foll: *Work 3 sts before patt rep box, rep 8-st patt 9 (9, 9, 10) times, work 3 sts after patt rep box. Cont in patt from chart and *at the same time* inc 1 st on each side of end-of-rnd m (1 st in from m) every 4 rnds 28 (20, 20, 18) times, then every 3 rnds 2 (15, 15, 20) time(s), working new sts into chart patt, ending with Rnd 7 (14, 14, 7) of chart and changing to shorter cir needle in larger size when there are too many sts to fit on

sts free for boatneck opening, and allowing welts to stand up on either side of seam (shoulder seam will be in the "valley" between the back and front welt as shown in photograph). Sew sleeves into armholes, stretching slightly to fit, sewing between the first patt st and outermost steek st on the body, and sewing just below the purled rnd at the top of the sleeve so purled sleeve sts do not show on RS of garment; sew through all layers at the welts. Sew facings at top of sleeves invisibly on WS to conceal cut edges of steeks. Weave in loose ends.

INCA JACKET

This zippered jacket is a study
of small repeating motifs.

Finished Size
About 34 (37¾, 41½, 45¼)" (86.5 [96, 105.5, 115] cm) bust circumference, zipped. Sweater shown photographed flat measures 41½"
(105.5 cm).

Yarn
About 175 (200, 225, 250) grams of a dark pattern color (A), 125
(150, 175, 200) grams each of two additional colors for body and
sleeves (B and C), 40 (50, 60, 70) grams of a light color (D), and 10
(15, 20, 25) grams each of two accent colors (E and F) of fingering-weight (#1 Super Fine) yarn.

Shown here
For sweaters both on model and photographed flat:
Isager Alpaca 2 (50% merino, 50% alpaca; 270 yd [247 m]/50 g):
#011 steel blue (A), 4 (4, 5, 5) skeins.

For sweater on model: Isager Alpaca 2 (50% merino, 50% alpaca;

270 yd [247 m]/50 g): #284 light brown heather (B) and #408 medium brown heather (C), 3 (3, 4, 4) skeins each; #201 tan heather (D),
1 (1, 2, 2) skein(s); #014 orange (E) and #023 blue (F), 1 skein each.

For sweater photographed flat: Isager Alpaca 2 (50% merino, 50%
alpaca; 270 yd [247 m]/50 g): #012 grayed olive (B), 3 (3, 4, 4) skeins;
#016 chartreuse (D), 1 (1, 2, 2) skein(s); #201 tan heather (E) and #015
salmon (F), 1 skein each.

Isager Wool 1 (100% wool; 340 yd [310 m]/50 g): #052s plum
heather (C), 3 (3, 4, 4) skeins.

Needles
Body and sleeves—size U.S. 4 (3.5 mm): 16" and 24" (40 and 60 cm)
circular (cir) and set of 4 or 5 double-pointed (dpn). *Lower edging,
neckband, and cuff facings*—size U.S. 1 (2.5 mm): 16" and 24" (40
and 60 cm) cir and set of 4 or 5 dpn. Adjust needle size if necessary
to obtain the correct gauge.

Notions

Markers (m); stitch holders, tapestry needle; 18 (18, 21, 22)" (45.5 [45.5, 53.5, 56] cm) separating zipper; sharp-point sewing needle or sewing machine; contrasting basting thread; matching sewing thread.

Gauge

34 stitches and 39 rounds = 4" (10 cm) in stranded two-color pattern from chart on larger needles, worked in rounds; 29 stitches and 41 rows = 4" (10 cm) in solid-color stockinette stitch on larger needles, worked in rounds.

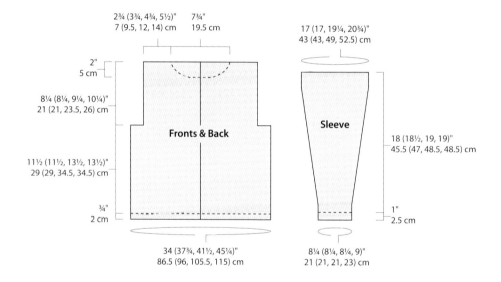

2¾ (3¾, 4¾, 5½)"
7 (9.5, 12, 14) cm

7¾"
19.5 cm

17 (17, 19¼, 20¾)"
43 (43, 49, 52.5) cm

2"
5 cm

8¼ (8¼, 9¼, 10¼)"
21 (21, 23.5, 26) cm

Fronts & Back

Sleeve

18 (18½, 19, 19)"
45.5 (47, 48.5, 48.5) cm

11½ (11½, 13½, 13½)"
29 (29, 34.5, 34.5) cm

¾"
2 cm

1"
2.5 cm

34 (37¾, 41½, 45¼)"
86.5 (96, 105.5, 115) cm

8¼ (8¼, 8¼, 9)"
21 (21, 21, 23) cm

NOTES

- This sweater is worked partially in stranded two-color knitting (see page 26).

- The body is worked in the round to the shoulders with steeks for the center front and armhole openings. The front neck shaping is stitched and cut during finishing. The sleeves are worked in the round in solid-color stockinette with facings at the upper edges to cover the raw edges of the steeked armhole openings.

POCKET LININGS

With C and larger needles, CO 38 sts. Work in St st for 4 (4, 5¼, 5¼)" (10 [10, 13.5, 13.5] cm). Place sts on holder. Work a second pocket lining in the same manner.

BODY

With A and longer smaller cir needle, CO 286 (318, 350, 382) sts. Work lower edging back and forth in rows as foll:

Row 1: (RS) *K2 with A, k2 with E; rep from * to last 2 sts, k2 with A.

Row 2: (WS) *P2 with A, p2 with E; rep from * to last 2 sts, p2 with A.

Rep Rows 1 and 2 until piece measures 1½" (3.8 cm) from CO, ending with a WS row. **Note:** Lower edging will be folded in half and hemmed during finishing and will contribute only ¾" (2 cm) toward finished lower body length shown on schematic. Change to longer, larger cir needle. With RS facing, use the backward-loop method (see Glossary) with A and C to CO 5 front steek sts onto left-hand needle, alternating 1 st of each color—5 steek sts added. On the foll rnds, work steek sts in a solid color, 1×1 checkerboard patt, or stripes, as you prefer in order to distinguish them from the patt sts. Place marker (pm) and join for working in rnds; rnd beg at start of steek sts.

Next rnd: (RS, counts as Rnd 1 of chart) With C, work 5 steek sts, pm, knit to end inc 3 sts evenly spaced—289 (321, 353, 385) patt sts, 5 steek sts.

Next rnd: Using A for patt color and C for background color, work 5 steek sts, then rep 32-st patt from Rnd 2 of Inca Jacket chart 9 (10, 11, 12) times, work 1 st at end of chart.

Cont in patt, work Rnds 3–20 of chart once, then work Rnds 1–20 once, then work Rnds 1–10 again 0 (0, 1, 1) time—40 (40, 50, 50) chart rnds completed; piece measures about 4 (4, 5¼, 5¼)" (10 [10, 13.5, 13.5] cm) above lower edging.

Next rnd: Change to F for colorway of sweater photographed flat or E for colorway of sweater on model and knit 1 rnd.

Next rnd: (insert pockets) With F or E according to your colorway, work 5 steek sts, k17 (21, 25, 29), *sl next 38 sts to holder, place 38 pocket lining sts on left-hand needle with RS facing, knit across 38 pocket sts,* knit to last 55 (59, 63, 67) sts; rep from * to * once more for second pocket, k17 (21, 25, 29) to end.

Using A for patt color and B for background color and keeping steek sts as established, work Rnds 11–20 of chart 0 (0, 1, 1) time, then rep Rnds 1–20 of chart 3 times, then work Rnds 1–10 of chart 1 time—70 (70, 80, 80) chart rnds completed above pocket insertion; piece measures about 11½ (11½, 13½, 13½)" (29 [29, 34.5, 34.5] cm) above lower edging.

Armhole Steeks

Work 5 front steek sts, cont in chart patt across 57 (65, 73, 81) sts for right front, BO 31 sts for right armhole, work until there are 113 (129, 145, 161) back sts on the needle after the BO gap, BO next 31 sts for

Inca Jacket

Legend:
- × A
- ☐ B, C, D, E, or F (see instructions)
- ☐ pattern repeat

left armhole, work 57 (65, 73, 81) left front sts after BO gap to end.

Next rnd: Work 5 front steek sts, cont in chart patt work to right armhole BO gap, *pm, use the backward-loop method to CO 5 steek sts alternating 1 st of each color, pm,* work in established patt to next BO gap; rep from * to * for second steek, work in patt to end for left front—242 (274, 306, 338) sts total; 57 (65, 73, 81) sts each front; 113 (129, 145, 161) back sts; 5 sts each in 3 steeks.

Cont in patt until 40 (40, 50, 60) rnds have been completed from start of armhole steeks, ending with Rnd 10 (10, 20, 10) of chart. Change to E for background color shown on sweater photographed flat or F for background color shown on model's sweater and work 10 rnds in patt. Change to D for background color for both versions and work 30 more rnds in patt, ending with Rnd 10 (10, 20, 10) of chart—80

(80, 90, 100) rnds completed from start of armhole steeks; armholes measure about 8¼ (8¼, 9¼, 10¼)" (21, [21, 23.5, 26] cm). Break yarns. Place steek sts on holders. Place 24 (32, 40, 48) shoulder sts at armhole edges of both fronts and back on holders, then place rem 33 sts of each front and 65 center back sts on separate holders. **Note:** The measurements on the schematic correspond to the above distribution of the neck and shoulder stitches and represent the designer's intended fit. The 41½" (105.5 cm) sweater shown photographed flat has a narrower neck opening with 49 sts across the back neck, 25 stitches in each front neck, and 48 stitches at each shoulder; these proportions are not shown on the schematic.

SLEEVES

With C and smaller dpn, CO 60 (60, 60, 66) sts. Arrange sts as evenly as possible on 3 or 4 dpn, pm, and join for working in rnds, being careful not to twist sts. Work in St st for 1" (2.5 cm). Change to larger dpn. Work in St st until piece measures 2" (5 cm) from CO. **Note:** This section of the cuff will be folded in half and hemmed during finishing and will contribute only 1" (2.5 cm) toward finished sleeve length shown on schematic.

Inc rnd: K1, M1 (see Glossary), knit to last st, M1, k1—2 sts inc'd.

Cont in St st and *at the same time* rep the inc rnd every 5 rnds 18 (25, 0, 0) times, then every 4 rnds 13 (6, 39, 30) times, then every 3 rnds 0 (0, 0, 11) times, changing to 16" (40 cm) cir needle when there are too many sts to fit on dpn—124 (124, 140, 150) sts. Work even in St st until sleeve measures 17 (17½, 18, 18)" (43 [44.5, 45.5, 45.5] cm) from CO. Change to working back and forth in rows. Work in St st in rows until piece measures 20 (20½, 21, 21)" (51 [52, 53.5, 53.5] cm) from CO, ending with a WS row. Knit 1 WS row to mark start of armhole facing, then cont in St st for ⅝" (1.5 cm) for facing. BO all sts.

FINISHING

Carefully steam press pieces to measurements under a damp cloth. **Note:** Sleeve is shown in the round on the schematic even though the final 2" (5 cm) is worked in rows below the facing turning ridge; armhole facings are not shown on schematic.

Steeks

Baste a line of contrasting thread along the center of each 5-st steek at armholes and center front.

With sewing machine or by hand, sew a line of small straight stitches one stitch away on each side of the basting line. Sew over the same two lines of stitching again. Carefully cut open each armhole and center front along the basting line.

Front Neck

Join 24 (32, 40, 48) shoulder sts of back and front using the three-needle bind-off method (see Glossary)—65 held center back sts and 33 held sts for each front rem. Measure down 2" (5 cm) at center front edges. Baste the outline of a curved neck opening on each front as shown by dotted line on schematic, beg the curves at the edges of the live front neck sts. Sew two lines of small straight stitches along the basting line. Cut out the neck shaping about ¼" (6 mm) inside the basting line to leave a small seam allowance.

Pockets

Place 38 held front pocket sts on smaller needle and with RS facing, rejoin F for sweater photographed flat or E for sweater on model. Work 3 rows in St st for pocket welt, beg and ending with a RS row. BO all sts with WS facing. Fold pocket welt in half to WS, and sew BO edge invisibly in place on WS. Sew short seams at pocket welt selvedges and tack sides of welt to front. Work second welt in the same manner. With C threaded on a tapestry needle, sew sides and bottom of each pocket lining to WS of front.

Neckband and Zipper Facing

Note: Pick up or work sts for neckband alternating 2 sts with A, then 2 sts with E, and end by picking

up 2 sts with A. Pick up below the sewing line along cut edges so neckline stitching does not show on RS of garment. Using shorter smaller cir needle, with RS facing and beg at right front edge, pick up and knit 33 sts along right front neck, knit across 65 held back neck sts dec 1 st in center, then pick up and knit 33 sts along left front neck edge—130 sts total. Work Rows 1 and 2 in vertical stripes as for lower body for 1½" (3.8 cm), beg and ending with WS Row 2.

Next row: (RS) Work 10 sts in established stripe patt, join second strand of A, BO center 110 sts, join second strand of E and work in established stripe patt to end—10 sts at each side for zipper facings.

With A threaded on a tapestry needle, sew 110 BO sts in center to pick-up row, then sew short selvedges at each end of neckband. Working 10 sts at each side separately, cont in stripe patt until zipper facings reach to the first chart row at bottom of fronts when slightly stretched. Place sts on separate holders.

Zipper
Fold front steek sts to WS. Pin zipper to front opening so zipper teeth show between folded front edges, top of zipper is aligned with pick-up row of neckband, and bottom of zipper is aligned with top row of striped lower body edging. Baste zipper in place as described on page 157. With sewing needle and matching thread, sew in zipper with small backstitches placed close to front fold lines on the right side. With sewing needle and thread, sew selvedges of facings to zipper tape on WS, taking care

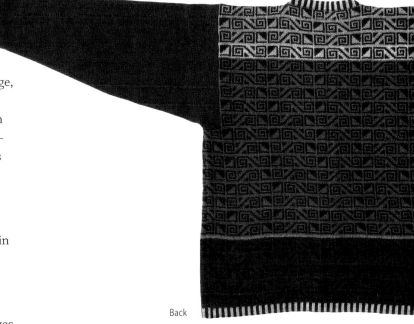

Back

that facing does not catch in zipper, and adding or removing rows at end of facings to achieve the correct fit. BO facing sts.

Sew sleeves into armholes, sewing between the patt st and outermost steek st on the body and sewing just below the purled ridge at the top of the sleeve so purled sleeve sts do not show on RS of garment. Sew facings at tops of sleeves invisibly on WS to conceal cut edges of steeks. Sew short selvedges at tops of sleeves to BO sts at base of armholes. Fold lower body striped edging in half to WS and sew invisibly in place, then sew short selvedges at each end of edging. Fold lower 1" (2.5 cm) of each sleeve cuff to WS and sew invisibly in place. Weave in loose ends. Steam-press seams carefully.

INDIANA

Large chevrons contrast with small scroll motifs in this zip-front pullover designed for a man.

Finished Size
About 34 (40½, 45½, 49½)" (86.5 [103, 115.5, 125.5] cm) chest circumference. Sweater shown photographed flat measures 45½" (115.5 cm).

Yarn
About 100 (125, 150, 175) grams each of two colors (A and B), 75 (100, 125, 150) grams of a third color (C), and 70 (80, 90, 100) grams of a fourth color (D) of fingering-weight (#1 Super Fine) yarn. About 50 grams each of three colors (E, F, and G) of the same or a different fingering-weight yarn.

Shown here
For sweaters both on model and photographed flat: Isager Highland (100% wool; 305 yd (279 m)/50 g): Scots pine (A), 2 (3, 3, 4) skeins; Tobacco (C), 2 (2, 3, 3) skeins.

Isager Alpaca 2 (50% merino, 50% alpaca; 270 yd [247 m]/50 g): #014 orange (E), #201 tan heather (F), and wine (G; discontinued), 1 skein each.

For sweater on model: Isager Highland (100% wool; 305 yd (279 m)/50 g): Oxford (B), 2 (3, 3, 4) skeins.

Isager Alpaca 2 (50% merino, 50% alpaca; 270 yd [247 m]/50 g): #020 teal (D), 2 skeins for all sizes.

For sweater photographed flat: Isager Highland (100% wool; 305 yd (279 m)/50 g): Oxford (used for both B and D), 4 (5, 5, 6) skeins.

Needles
Body and sleeves—size U.S. 3 (3.0 mm): 24" or 32" (60 or 80 cm) circular (cir). *Facings and neckband*—size U.S. 1 (2.5 mm): two 24" or 32" (60 or 80 cm) cir. Adjust needle size if necessary to obtain the correct gauge.

Notions
Tapestry needle; stitch holder; 8 (9, 9, 10)" (20.5 [23, 23, 25.5] cm) zipper; sharp-point sewing needle, contrasting basting thread, and matching sewing thread (for attaching zipper).

Gauge
29 stitches and 39 rows = 4" (10 cm) in stockinette stitch on larger needle.

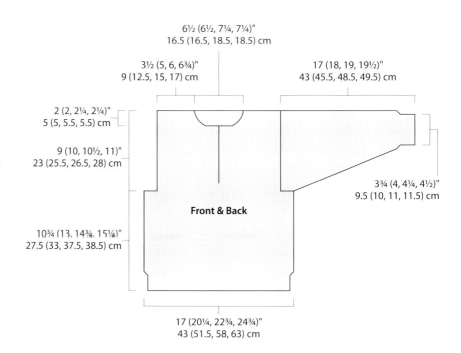

STITCH GUIDE

Triangles

(multiple of 6 sts + 1)

Row 1: (RS) *K1 with A, k5 with G; rep from * to last st, k1 with A.

Row 2: (WS) K1 with A, p1 with A, *p3 with G, p3 with A; rep from * to last 5 sts, p3 with G, p1 with A, k1 with A.

Row 3: K3 with A, *k1 with G, k5 with A; rep from * to last 4 sts, k1 with G, k3 with A.

Vertical Stripes

(multiple of 4 sts + 2)

Row 1: (RS) *K2 with first color, k2 with second color; rep from * to last 2 sts, k2 with first color.

Row 2: (WS) [K1, p1] with first color, *p2 with second color, p2 with first color; rep from * to last 4 sts, p2 with second color, [p1, k1] with first color.

Repeat Rows 1 and 2 for patt. See instructions for colors.

Schematic measurements:

6½ (6½, 7¼, 7¼)"
16.5 (16.5, 18.5, 18.5) cm

3½ (5, 6, 6¾)"
9 (12.5, 15, 17) cm

17 (18, 19, 19½)"
43 (45.5, 48.5, 49.5) cm

2 (2, 2¼, 2¼)"
5 (5, 5.5, 5.5) cm

9 (10, 10½, 11)"
23 (25.5, 26.5, 28) cm

3¾ (4, 4¼, 4½)"
9.5 (10, 11, 11.5) cm

Front & Back

10¾ (13, 14¾, 15¼)"
27.5 (33, 37.5, 38.5) cm

17 (20¼, 22¾, 24¾)"
43 (51.5, 58, 63) cm

NOTES

- The back and front are worked in rows from the top down in separate pieces, using plain stockinette, intarsia (see page 53), and stranded two-color knitting (see page 26). After completing the front and back and joining the shoulders, the sleeve stitches are picked up along the armhole edge and worked in rows down to the cuffs.

- Knit the first and last stitch of every row for garter selvedges stitches. These garter edge stitches are included in the Triangles and Vertical Stripes patterns.

- The sweater shown photographed flat uses the same color (Oxford) for both B and D.

- The chart for the sweater shown photographed flat (Labyrinth Option 1) and the chart for the sweater shown on the model (Labyrinth Option 2) are variations of one another with the colors reversed. They are interchangeable, and you may use the same chart throughout or a combination of both charts as you prefer.

BACK

With E and larger needle, CO 97 (121, 139, 151) sts. Knitting the first and last sts of each row (see Notes), work 4 rows in St st, ending with a RS row.

Next row: (WS) With G, k1, purl to last st, k1.

With A and G, work Rows 1–3 of Triangle patt (see Stitch Guide), beg and ending with a RS row. With A, work even in St st with garter edge sts until piece measures 3 (2¾, 2¼, 2¼)" (7.5 [7, 5.5, 5.5] cm) from CO, ending with a WS row. With B, prepare 2 bobbins or butterflies. Using a separate strand of yarn for each color section and twisting yarns around each other at color changes to prevent holes from forming, establish colors for upper chevron patt as foll: (RS) K1 with B, knit to last st with A, k1 with B using second yarn butterfly.

Next row: (WS) K1 with B, p1 with B, purl to last 2 sts with A, p1 with B, k1 with B.

Work 46 (58, 67, 73) more rows in this manner, working 1 more st with B at each side every row until 1 center A st rem, ending with a WS (WS, RS, RS) row. With B, work 0 (0, 1, 1) WS row, inc 0 (0, 0, 2) sts evenly—97 (121, 139, 153) sts; piece measures about 8 (9, 9½, 10)" (20.5 [23, 24, 25.5] cm) from CO. Beg and ending where indicated for your size, work Rows 1–10 from the Labyrinth chart of your choice (see Notes)—piece measures about 9 (10, 10½, 11)" (23 [25.5, 26.5, 28] cm) from CO. Cut yarns.

Shape Armholes

With C, prepare 2 bobbins or butterflies. With a separate butterfly for each group of CO sts, use the backward-loop method (see Glossary) to CO 13 sts with C at each end of needle—123 (147, 165, 179) sts. Establish colors for lower chevron patt by deliberately working another WS row as foll: (WS) K1 with C, p12 with C, purl to last 13 sts with B, p12 with C, k1 with C.

Next row: (RS) K14 with C, knit to last 14 sts with B, k14 with C.

Work 47 (59, 68, 75) more rows in this manner, working 1 more st with C at each side every row until 1 center B st rem, ending with a WS (WS, RS, WS) row—lower body measures about 5 (6¼, 7¼, 8)" (12.5 [16, 18.5, 20.5] cm) from armhole CO. Work even in St st with C until lower body measures 8¾ (11, 12¾, 13¼)" (22 [28, 32.5, 33.5] cm) from armhole CO, or 2" (5 cm) less than desired length, ending with a WS row.

Lower Edging

Knit 1 RS row, dec 25 (29, 35, 37) sts evenly spaced—98 (118, 130, 142) sts. Change to D (see Notes) and work in St st for 1¾" (4.5 cm) from dec row, ending with a WS row. Change to smaller needle. With B for first color and E for second color, work Vertical Stripes patt (see Stitch Guide) for 2¼" (5.5 cm)—piece measures about 4" (10 cm) from dec row. **Note:** Lower edging will be folded in half and hemmed during finishing and will contribute only 2" (5) toward finished lower body length shown on schematic; ¼" (6 mm) of stripe patt will show on RS above fold line. BO all sts.

FRONT

Right Front Neck

With E and larger needle, CO 25 (37, 43, 49) sts. Knitting the first and last sts of each row, work 4 rows in St st, ending with a RS row.

Next row: (WS) With G, k1, purl to last st, k1.

With A and G, work Rows 1–3 of Triangle patt (see Stitch Guide), beg and ending with a RS row. Cont in St st with A, at neck edge (beg of WS rows) CO 1 st 2 times, then CO 3 sts 2 (2, 3, 3) times, then CO 5 sts 1 time, then CO 10 sts 1 time—48 (60, 69, 75) sts. With A, work even in St st with 1 garter edge st at armhole edge (beg of RS rows; end of WS rows) and 3 garter edge sts at neck edge (end of RS rows, beg of WS rows) until piece measures 3 (2¾, 2¼, 2¼)" (7.5 [7, 5.5, 5.5] cm) from CO, ending with a WS row. Prepare one bobbin or butterfly with B. Establish colors for upper chevron patt as foll: (RS) K1 with B, knit to end with A.

Next row: (WS) K3 with A, purl to last 2 sts with A, p1 with B, k1 with B.

Keeping 3 sts at neck edge and 1 st at armhole in garter st, work 46 (58, 67, 73) more rows in this manner, working 1 more st with B every row until no A sts rem, and ending with a WS (WS, RS, RS) row. With B, work 0 (0, 1, 1) WS row, inc 0 (0, 0, 1) st—48 (60, 69, 76) sts; piece measures about 8 (9, 9½, 10)" (20.5 [23, 24, 25.5] cm) from CO. Break yarn and place sts on holder.

Left Front Neck

Work as for right front neck until Triangle patt has been completed, ending with a RS row—25 (37, 43, 49) sts. Cont in St st with A, work 1 WS row, then at neck edge (beg of RS rows) CO 1 st 2 times, then CO 3 sts 2 (2, 3, 3) times, then CO 5 sts 1 time, then CO 10 sts 1 time—48 (60, 69, 75) sts. With A, work even in St st with 1 garter edge st at armhole edge (end of RS rows; beg of WS rows) and 3 garter edge sts at neck edge (beg of RS rows; end of WS rows) until piece measures 3 (2¾, 2¼, 2¼)" (7.5 [7, 5.5, 5.5] cm) from CO, ending with a WS row. Prepare 1 bobbin or butterfly with B. Establish colors for upper chevron patt as foll: (RS) Knit to last st with A, k1 with B.

Next row: (WS) K1 with B, p1 with B, purl to last 3 sts with A, k3 with A.

Keeping 3 sts at neck edge and 1 st at armhole in garter st, work 46 (58, 67, 73) more rows in this manner, working 1 more st with B every row until no A sts rem and ending with a WS (WS, RS, RS) row. With B, work 0 (0, 1, 1) WS row, inc 0 (0, 0, 1) st—48 (60, 69, 76) sts; piece measures same as right front neck from CO. Break yarn and leave sts on needle.

Join Fronts

With RS facing, return 48 (60, 69, 76) held right front sts to larger needle so the right front sts will be worked first on the next row. Work Row 1 of your chosen Labyrinth chart over 48 (60, 69, 76) right front sts, use the backward-loop method to CO 1 st at center front, cont Row 1 of chart over 48 (60, 69,

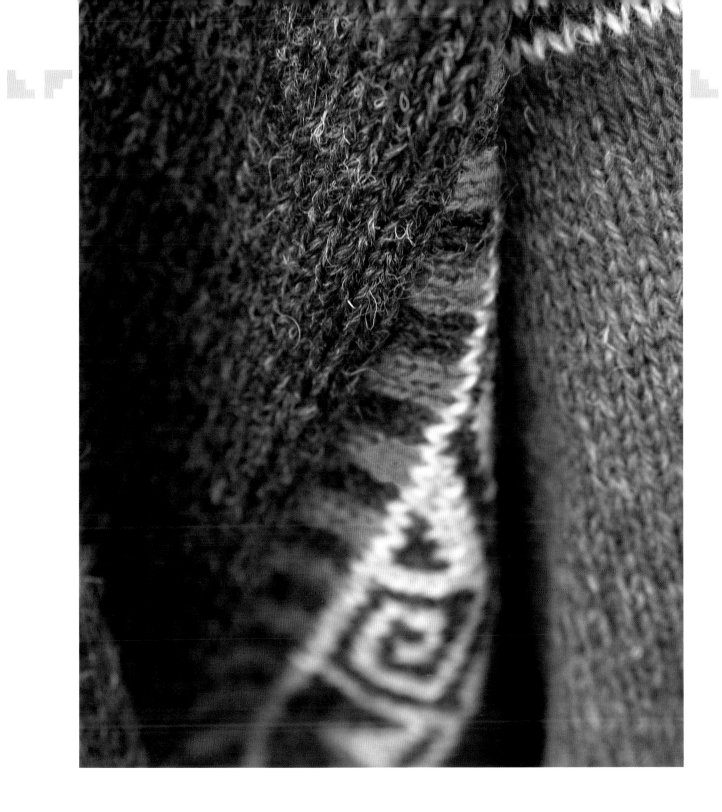

INDIANA

76) left front sts, ending where indicated for your size—97 (121, 139, 153) sts. Work Rows 2–10 of chart—piece measures about 9 (10, 10½, 11)" (23 [25.5, 26.5, 28] cm) from CO. Work armhole shaping, lower body, and lower edging as for back.

SLEEVES

With E threaded on a tapestry needle, sew shoulder seams. With B, larger needle, WS facing, and beg in the corner of one armhole notch, pick up and purl 67 (73, 79, 81) sts along armhole edge to shoulder seam, then 67 (73, 79, 81) sts to corner of other armhole notch—134 (146, 158, 162) sts total. With B and E, work 4 rows in Vertical Stripes patt, ending with a WS row. Work Row 1 of your chosen Labyrinth chart, dec 0 (0, 2, 2) sts evenly spaced—134 (146, 156, 160) sts rem. Work Rows 2–10 of chart, dec 1 (dec 1, inc 1, dec 3) st(s) in Row 10—133 (145, 157, 157) sts. With A and G, work Rows 1–3 of Triangle patt, beg and ending with a RS row—piece measures about 1¾" (4.5 cm) from pick-up row. With A, work in St st and *at the same time* dec 1 st each side inside garter edge st every 3 rows 24 (27, 30, 30) times, then every 4 rows 12 times—61 (67, 73, 73) sts rem. Work even in St st until piece measures 15 (16, 17, 17½)" (38 [40.5, 43, 44.5] cm) from pick-up row or 2" (5 cm) less than desired length, ending with a WS row.

Cuff Edging

Knit 1 RS row, dec 7 (9, 11, 7) sts evenly spaced—54 (58, 62, 66) sts rem. Change to D and work in St st for 1¾" (4.5) from dec row, ending with a WS row. Change to smaller needle. With B for first color and E

for second color, work Vertical Stripes patt for 2¼" (5.5 cm)—piece measures about 4" (10 cm) from dec row. **Note:** Cuff edging will be folded in half and hemmed during finishing and will contribute only 2" (5) toward finished sleeve length shown on schematic; ¼" (6 mm) of stripe patt will show on RS above fold line. BO all sts.

FINISHING

Neckband

With D, smaller needle, RS facing, and beg at right front neck edge, pick up and knit 35 (35, 40, 40) sts along right neck edge, 50 (50, 56, 56) sts across back neck, and 35 (35, 40, 40) sts along left neck edge—120 (120, 136, 136) sts total. Keeping 3 sts at each side in garter st, work in St st for 5 rows, beg and ending with a WS row. With WS facing, slip the second smaller needle into each purl bump of the neckband pick-up row; these loops are just picked up and placed on the needle, not picked up and knitted—120 (120, 136, 136) picked-up loops on second cir needle. Hold cir needles tog and parallel with RS of neckband facing, live sts of neckband on needle in front (working needle), and picked-up loops on needle in back.

Next row: (RS, welt row) With B, *insert right-hand tip of working needle into first st on both needles and k2tog (1 st from each needle); rep from * to complete welt—120 (120, 136, 136) sts total on working needle; no picked-up loops rem.

With D, work in St st with 3 garter sts at each side for 1" (2.5 cm) above welt row, ending with a WS row.

Labyrinth Option 1

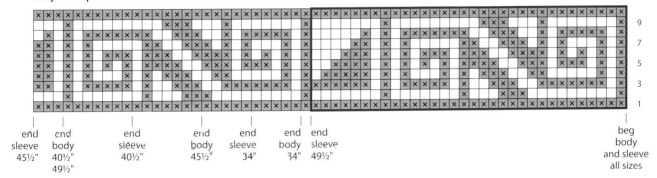

end	9
sleeve	7
45½"	5
end body 40½" 49½"	3
end sleeve 40½"	1

end sleeve 45½"   end body 40½" 49½"   end sleeve 40½"   end body 45½"   end sleeve 34"   end body 34"   end sleeve 49½"   beg body and sleeve all sizes

Labyrinth Option 2

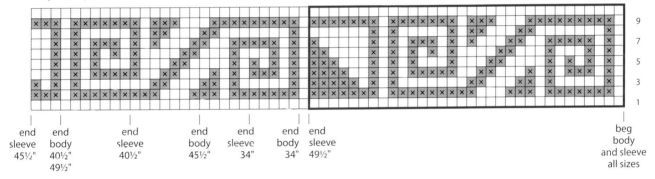

9
7
5
3
1

end sleeve 45½"   end body 40½" 49½"   end sleeve 40½"   end body 45½"   end sleeve 34"   end body 34"   end sleeve 49½"   beg body and sleeve all sizes

☒ B   ☐ F   ☐ pattern repeat

Note: In next stripe rows, use A for first color and D for second color for sweater shown photographed flat; use E for first color and D for second color for sweater shown on model.

Next row: (RS) K3 with D, work Row 1 of Vertical Stripes patt over center 114 (114, 130, 130) sts, k3 with D.

Keeping 3 garter sts at each side, work in established stripe patt for 2" (5 cm)—piece measures about 3" (7.5 cm) above welt row. **Note:** Neckband facing will be folded in half and hemmed to 1½" (3.8 cm) high above welt row during finishing; ½" (1.3 cm) of stripe patt will show on RS below fold line. Cont in St st with A for sweater shown photographed flat and D for sweater shown on model.

Back

10¼, 10¾)" (23 [25.5, 26, 27.5] cm) from fold line at top of neckband, or about 1½" (3.8 cm) below bottom of front neck slit. BO all sts, leaving facing extensions free for now.

Zipper

Pin zipper to front opening so zipper teeth show between garter edges of neck slit and top of zipper is aligned with fold line of neckband; bottom of zipper may extend below base of neck slit for some sizes. Baste zipper in place as described on page 157. With sewing needle and matching thread, sew in zipper with small backstitches placed close to selvedges of garter neck edging on the right side. With sewing needle and thread, sew selvedges of facing extensions to zipper tape on WS, taking care that facing does not catch in zipper.

Handwash sweater gently in lukewarm water. Squeeze out extra water by rolling in a towel or spinning in washing machine. Lay sweater out on towels over a carpet and pin to measurements. **Note:** Facings for lower body and cuffs are not shown on schematic.

Do not remove pins until sweater is completely dry. With matching color yarn threaded on a tapestry needle and using the mattress st (see Glossary), sew sleeve and side seams.

Fold lower body edging in half to WS and sew invisibly in place. Fold lower 2" (5 cm) of each sleeve cuff to WS and sew invisibly in place. Weave in loose ends.

Next row: (RS) K35 (35, 40, 40) sts join second strand of yarn, BO center 50 (50, 56, 56) sts, knit to end—35 (35, 40, 40) sts rem at each side.

Fold neckband in half, and with yarn threaded on a tapestry needle, sew BO sts in center of facing to pick-up row of back neck on WS. Working each side separately, cont in St st with 3 garter edge sts and *at the same time* dec 1 st each side of center gap every 3 rows 8 (18, 10, 15) times, then every 2 rows 17 (7, 20, 15) times—10 sts rem at each side. Work even as established until facing measures 9 (10,

SHORT-ROW SHAPING

Short-rows allow you to add rows (and therefore length) to a group of stitches on the needles—not all of the stitches are worked all the way across every row. Short-rows are commonly used to create diagonal shapes, such as the sloped shoulders on garments. The key to short-rows is to hide the gap or hole that's created when the worked is turned in the middle of a row.

When working short-rows, work the required number of stitches to the turning point, turn the work around so the other side is facing you, make a yarnover, then work back. On a subsequent row, work the yarnover with an adjacent stitch to close the gap that was created at the turning point. Short-rows can begin on either right-side or wrong-side rows. The example here has the turning point worked four stitches from the end of the row. Do not include yarnovers in the stitch count—they will be used later to close the gaps.

Beginning on a Right-Side Row

With the right-side facing, knit to the turning point, turn the work around so that the wrong side is facing you, make a yarnover on the right needle (Figure 1), then purl to the end. The yarnover will occupy the gap formed at the turning point and there will now be two more rows of knitting on these stitches (Figure 2). On the next right-side row, knit to the gap, then work the yarnover together with the stitch on the other side of the gap (Figure 3) to close the hole.

Beginning on a Wrong-Side Row

With the wrong-side facing, purl to the turning point, turn the work around so that the right side is facing you, make a yarnover on the right needle (Figure 4), then knit to the end. The yarnover will occupy the gap formed at the turning point and there will now be two more rows of knitting on these stitches (Figure 5). On the next wrong-side row, purl to the gap, then purl the yarnover together with the next stitch through the back loop (Figure 6).

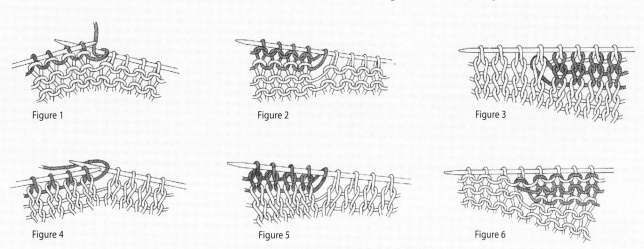

Figure 1   Figure 2   Figure 3

Figure 4   Figure 5   Figure 6

ABBREVIATIONS

beg(s)	begin(s); beginning		**rep**	repeat(s); repeating
BO	bind off		**rev St st**	reverse stockinette stitch
CC	contrasting color		**rnd(s)**	round(s)
cm	centimeter(s)		**RS**	right side
cn	cable needle		**sl**	slip
CO	cast on		**sl st**	slip st (slip 1 stitch purlwise unless otherwise indicated)
cont	continue(s); continuing			
dec(s)	decrease(s); decreasing		**ssk**	slip 2 stitches knitwise, one at a time, from the left needle to right needle, insert left needle tip through both front loops and knit together from this position (1 stitch decrease)
dpn	double-pointed needles			
foll	follow(s); following			
g	gram(s)			
inc(s)	increase(s); increasing			
k	knit			
k1f&b	knit into the front and back of same stitch		**st(s)**	stitch(es)
			St st	stockinette stitch
kwise	knitwise, as if to knit		**tbl**	through back loop
m	marker(s)		**tog**	together
MC	main color		**WS**	wrong side
mm	millimeter(s)		**wyb**	with yarn in back
M1	make one (increase)		**wyf**	with yarn in front
p	purl		**yd**	yard(s)
p1f&b	purl into front and back of same stitch		**yo**	yarnover
			*	repeat starting point
patt(s)	pattern(s)		*** ***	repeat all instructions between asterisks
psso	pass slipped stitch over			
pwise	purlwise, as if to purl		**( )**	alternate measurements and/or instructions
rem	remain(s); remaining			
			[ ]	work instructions as a group a specified number of times

GLOSSARY

BIND-OFFS

Standard Bind-Off

Knit the first stitch, *knit the next stitch (two stitches on right needle), insert left needle tip into first stitch on right needle *(Figure 1)* and lift this stitch up and over the second stitch *(Figure 2)* and off the needle *(Figure 3)*. Repeat from * for the desired number of stitches.

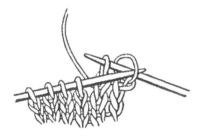

Figure 1

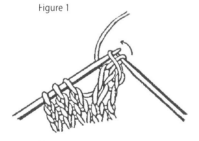

Figure 2

Figure 3

Three-Needle Bind-Off

Place the stitches to be joined onto two separate needles and hold the needles parallel so that the right sides of knitting face together. Insert a third needle into the first stitch on each of two needles *(Figure 1)* and knit them together as one stitch *(Figure 2)*, *knit the next stitch on each needle the same way, then use the left needle tip to lift the first stitch over the second and off the needle *(Figure 3)*. Repeat from * until no stitches remain on first two needles. Cut yarn and pull tail through last stitch to secure.

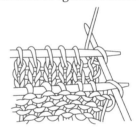

Figure 1

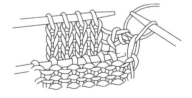

Figure 2

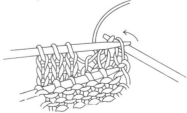

Figure 3

CAST-ONS

Backward-Loop Cast-On

*Loop working yarn and place it on needle backward so that it doesn't unwind. Repeat from *.

Knitted Cast-On

Make a slipknot of working yarn and place it on the left needle if there are no stitches already there. *Use the right needle to knit the first stitch (or slipknot) on left needle (*Figure 1*) and place new loop onto left needle to form a new stitch (*Figure 2*). Repeat from * for the desired number of stitches, always working into the last stitch made.

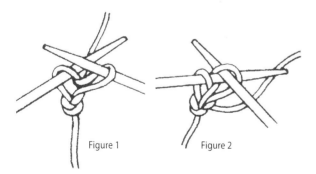

Figure 1   Figure 2

Long-Tail (Continental) Cast-On

Leaving a long tail (about ½" [1.3 cm] for each stitch to be cast on), make a slipknot and place on right needle. Place thumb and index finger of your left hand between the yarn ends so that working yarn is around your index finger and tail end is around your thumb and secure the yarn ends with your other fingers. Hold your palm upward, making a V of yarn (*Figure 1*). *Bring needle up through loop on thumb (*Figure 2*), catch first strand around index finger, and go back down through loop on thumb (*Figure 3*). Drop loop off thumb and, placing thumb back in V configuration, tighten resulting stitch on needle (*Figure 4*). Repeat from * for the desired number of stitches.

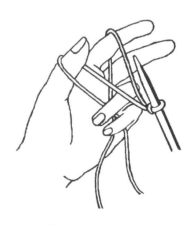

Figure 1

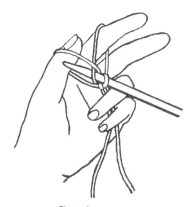

Figure 2

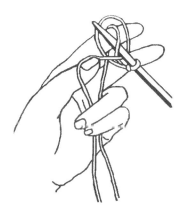

Figure 3

Figure 4

CROCHET

Single Crochet (sc)

*Insert hook into the second chain from the hook (or the next stitch), yarn over hook and draw through a loop, yarn over hook (*Figure 1*), and draw it through both loops on hook (*Figure 2*). Repeat from * for the desired number of stitches.

Figure 1

Figure 2

Slip-stitch Crochet (sl st)

*Insert hook into stitch, yarn over hook and draw a loop through both the stitch and the loop already on hook. Repeat from * for the desired number of stitches.

DECREASES

Slip, Slip, Knit (ssk)

Slip two stitches individually knitwise *(Figure 1)*, insert left needle tip into the front of these two slipped stitches, and use the right needle to knit them together through their back loops *(Figure 2)*.

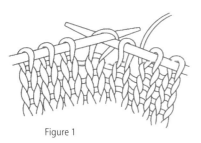

Figure 1

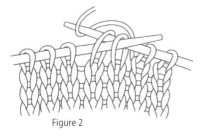

Figure 2

GAUGE

Measuring Gauge

Gauge swatches are necessary both to learn the pattern stitch and to verify that you are knitting with the correct tension to achieve the given dimensions of the garment.

Knit a swatch at least 4" (10 cm) square with the needles and stitch pattern specified. Remove the stitches from the needles or bind them off loosely. Dampen the swatch, block it on a damp cloth (such as a pressing cloth), and pin it to shape. Do not remove the pins until the swatch is completely dry. Place the dry swatch on a flat surface. Place a ruler over the swatch and count the number of stitches across and number of rows down (including fractions of stitches and rows) in 2" (5 cm) and divide this number by two to get the number of stitches (including fractions of stitches) in one inch. Repeat two or three times on different areas of the swatch to confirm the measurements. If you have more stitches and rows than called for in the instructions, knit another swatch with larger needles; if you have fewer stitches and rows, knit another swatch with smaller needles.

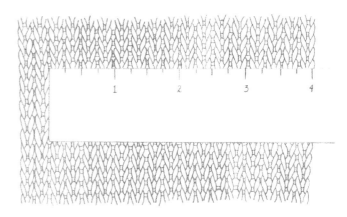

GRAFTING

Kitchener Stitch

Arrange stitches on two needles so that there is the same number of stitches on each needle. Hold the needles parallel to each other with wrong sides of the knitting together. Allowing about ½" (1.3 cm) per stitch to be grafted, thread matching yarn on a tapestry needle. Work from right to left as follows:

Step 1. Bring tapestry needle through the first stitch on the front needle as if to purl and leave the stitch on the needle *(Figure 1)*.

Step 2. Bring tapestry needle through the first stitch on the back needle as if to knit and leave that stitch on the needle *(Figure 2)*.

Step 3. Bring tapestry needle through the first front stitch as if to knit and slip this stitch off the needle, then bring tapestry needle through the next front stitch as if to purl and leave this stitch on the needle *(Figure 3)*.

Step 4. Bring tapestry needle through the first back stitch as if to purl and slip this stitch off the needle, then bring tapestry needle through the next back stitch as if to knit and leave this stitch on the needle *(Figure 4)*.

Repeat Steps 3 and 4 until one stitch remains on each needle, adjusting the tension to match the rest of the knitting as you go. To finish, bring tapestry needle through the front stitch as if to knit and slip this stitch off the needle, then bring tapestry needle through the back stitch as if to purl and slip this stitch off the needle.

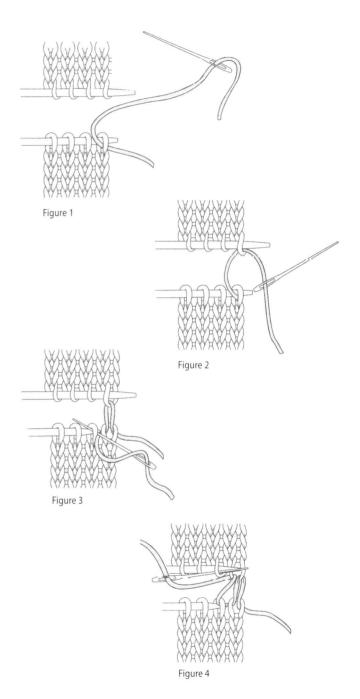

Figure 1

Figure 2

Figure 3

Figure 4

INCREASES

Raised Make-One (M1)

With left needle tip, lift the strand between the last knitted stitch and the first stitch on the left needle from front to back *(Figure 1)*, then knit the lifted loop through the back *(Figure 2)*.

Raised Make-One Purlwise (M1 pwise)

With left needle tip, lift the strand between the needles from front to back *(Figure 1)*, then purl the lifted loop through the back *(Figure 2)*.

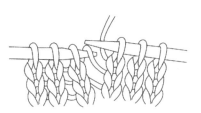

Figure 1

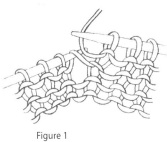

Figure 1

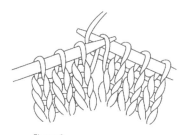

Figure 2

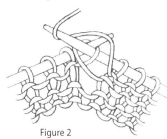

Figure 2

POM-POM

Cut out two circles of thick paper and cut a small hole in the center of each. Thread yarn around and around the paper "doughnut" until it is completely full. Cut the outer ends of the yarn by inserting the tips of the scissors between the two pieces of paper. Cut another piece of yarn and use it to bind together the strands between the pieces of paper, then tie it in a tight knot. Clip into the paper and pull it away. Carefully steam and fluff the pom-pom to fill it out.

SEAMS

Mattress Stitch

Place the pieces to be seamed on a table with right sides facing up. Begin at the lower edge and work upward as follows:

Insert threaded needle under one bar between the two edge stitches on one piece, then under the corresponding bar plus the bar above it on the other piece (Figure 1). *Pick up the next two bars on the first piece (Figure 2), then the next two bars on the other (Figure 3). Repeat from *, ending by picking up the last bar or pair of bars on the first piece.

To reduce bulk in the seam, pick up the bars in the center of the edge stitches instead of between the last two stitches.

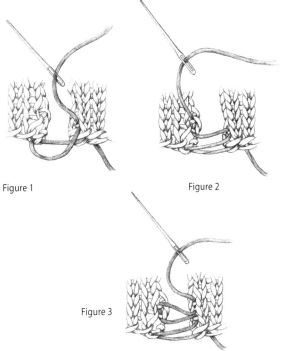

Figure 1   Figure 2

Figure 3

TASSEL

Cut out a piece of thick paper that measures about 1½" (4 cm) square. Wind a doubled strand of yarn about 20 times around the paper. Tie a length of yarn tightly around the strands at one end of the paper and then cut yarn *(Figure 1)*. Wrap the top of the tassel to secure it *(Figure 2)* and cut open the other end.

WASHING

Wash garment pieces before joining. Use a small amount of quality wool wash and warm water (it is important that the water be neither too hot nor too cold). Let the garment soak for 20 minutes. Gently squeeze out the water (do not twist or wring), then rinse with water of the same temperature. Gently squeeze out the water, place the garment in a nylon net bag, and run it through the spin-only cycle of the washing machine. Lay it on top of a towel on a flat surface, pat it to the correct dimensions, and pin it in place. Allow it to air-dry thoroughly before removing the pins.

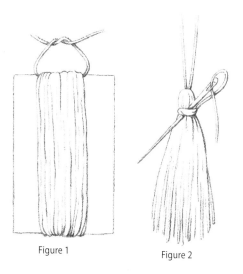

Figure 1

Figure 2

ZIPPER

With right side facing and zipper closed,
pin zipper to the knitted pieces so edges cover
the zipper teeth. With contrasting thread and
right side facing, baste zipper in place close
to teeth *(Figure 1)*. Turn work over and with
matching sewing thread and needle, stitch
outer edges of zipper to wrong side of knitting
(Figure 2), being careful to follow a single column of stitches in the knitting to keep zipper
straight. Turn work back to right side facing,
and with matching sewing thread, sew knitted
fabric close to teeth *(Figure 3)*. Remove basting.

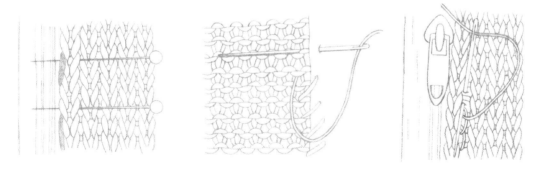

Figure 1   Figure 2   Figure 3

INDEX

SOURCES

All yarns distributed in the United States by:

Tutto Santa Fe
137 W. Water St., Ste. 220
Santa Fe, NM 87501
tuttosantafe.com

ALSO AVAILABLE FROM DESIGNER MARIANNE ISAGER

**Japanese Inspired Knits:
Marianne Isager Collection**
$22.95, ISBN 978-1-59668-114-9

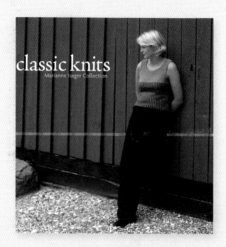

**Classic Knits:
Marianne Isager Collection**
$24.95, ISBN 978-1-59668-115-6

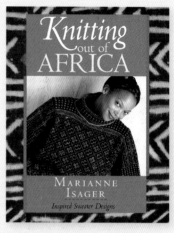

**Knitting Out of Africa:
Inspired Sweater Designs**
$24.95, ISBN 978-1-931499-98-9

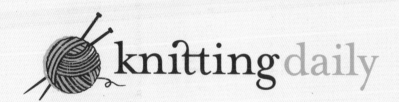